The Language of Hope

*Reclaiming the heart's language to create
a post-pandemic future our young
people can believe in*

Jeanette Pritchard

ISBN: PBK: 978-0-6489676-0-6;
eBook: 978-0-6489676-1-3

First paperback edition October 2020.

Editing and layout: Claire McGregor, Kookaburra Hill Publishing Services.

Cover artwork: 'River Red Gum' from Yea, Victoria, by artist Kaylie Rogers. *Trees symbolise resilience and hope and provide safety and nourishment. They have the power to inspire and express our deepest feelings of love, gratitude and happiness. Kaylie Rogers has painted a Red River Gum on the edge of the river, soaking the water of the river, which is needed to sustain it. The water is a metaphor for heart energy needed by us to be truly human and to nourish our young people.*

Published by:

Jeanette Pritchard

www.theheartslanguage.com.au

For
Phillipa, Finn, Abi, Sam and James

Many of the things we need can wait. The child cannot.
Right now is the time his bones are being formed, his
blood is being made, and his senses are being developed.
To him we cannot answer 'Tomorrow,' his name is today.

Gabriela Mistral

Jeanette Pritchard's new book The Language of Hope *is nothing short of a summons back to the Beloved Community. With elegance and authority, she shines a light on the limits of our modern ways of organising our societies and economies, as well as calling out the counterfeit bill of goods that is 'individualism' and 'consumerism'. She offers us hope, shedding light on, and sounding a call to action towards a preferred future for those with most at stake: our young citizens; our children. The gift at the heart of this book is in Jeanette's unyielding belief in the inherent promise of every child to contribute to the wellbeing of their communities. Allied to this is her conviction that while 'the village' that is needed to raise each child may have become fragmented, our greatest hope is in restoring our local communities into the nests from which the promise of every child can hatch.*

Cormac Russell, Author of *Rekindling Democracy,*
A *Professional's* **Guide to Working** *in* **Citizen Space**

Jeanette Pritchard's work depicts the world's current condition – in need of desperate renovating. I am confident that this book will open your eyes to some of the rust and scuffs in society, and that there is a way to polish it up. I hope this book motivates you to help the future. I know Jeanette and, resultantly, I, will be heard. But I can only hope that it sticks with you, that being 'heard' actually means something.

Ciara Symons

The Language of Hope *truly offers hope for our people and our planet. Jeanette Pritchard has written a heartfelt call, not just to our young people but to all of us, to work together for a fair and just society. Her book touched my heart and brought tears to my eyes at times. The combination of Jeanette's readable and accessible picture of where we are at today, and how we came to be here, along with the stories of seven different women who are taking action now, makes for a powerful argument, and template, of what it is possible to achieve. And then there are the profound words of Ciara Symons; poetry that takes us beyond the constraints of our prosaic language to think, to feel and to understand from our hearts, our minds and our deepest selves.*

Kerry Willis

Jeanette Pritchard has done an enormous amount of research to show the situation we are in and uses creative suggestions on how we can improve. She has used inspirational and achievable success stories to show us what those changes can look like.

Jill Rigby

Acknowledgements

This book has emerged after many years of working with young people, observing the society we have created and coming to the strong opinion that we must do better. Now the book has finally seen the light of day, I would like to acknowledge the people who have made it possible:

My editor Claire McGregor for her wise and patient guidance. Kerry Willis for her thoughtful and incisive feedback. Jill Rigby and Jack Fryer for their support in the final stages of the book. Kaylie Rogers for her beautiful artwork for the cover. Ciara Symons for sharing her poetry and reflections on life. Cheryne Blom for her lovely meditation.

The wonderful women who were willing to share the stories of their projects to show it is possible to make change in this world if one has enough passion and determination: Marg Hepworth, Lea Trafford, Clare Pritchard, Donalea Patman, Shakti McLaren, Belinda Grooby and Judy Avisar.

The following writers who have given me permission to include their material: John Marsden, David Leser, Matt Fisher, The Climate Council. The wisdom of Kon Karapanagiotidis. His total commitment to vulnerable asylum seekers continually inspires me.

Many of the people I have worked with over the years in projects aimed at giving young people a positive future. I have learnt so much from all of them. These include: The Standing Tall mentoring program: Louise Yole, Rob Vecchiet, Val McDowell, Heather Ward, Renee Casey Manson; The Stride Foundation: Jane Hill, Jill Gustave Marston, Andrew Wicking, Ariana Sutton, Lyn Nicholson, Eleanor Cesari, Miranda Cerini; BigBrothersBigSisters Australia: Daniel Griffiths, Jessica Jones, Sarah Downie, Raffi Jones, Diana Ginger.

All the mentors in both the Standing Tall and Big Futures mentoring programs who showed the heart's language in action in the relationships they formed with young people in those programs.

Leaders who have inspired me with the amazing work they do in the world: Cormac Russell from Nurture Development; Peter Kenyon from Bank of Ideas; Michelle Dunscombe from the Jeder Institute; Gilbert Rochecouste from Village Well.

Fellow dreamers who want to make this world a better place: Dianne Dalley, Glenn Wills, Evi Van de Niet, David Adams, Robert Middendorp, Cheryne Blom, Phil Byers, Jonno Heard, Bill Brindle, Eva Migdal and Mike Clarke.

Local community leaders Aimee te Boekhorst, Teresa Schroder and Carmel Mitchell who 'walk the talk' and keep the spirit of my local community alive.

Dear friends who have given me moral support in writing this book: Paula Scott, Liz Waters, Carol Dyer, Ali Murphy, Karen Parish, Kate Holden, Heather Heard and Di Pettigrew.

My sister Margaret who has provided unfailing encouragement for my project. My brothers Leon and Colin and their wives Kate and Janet for their support over the years. My amazing children and their wonderful partners: Matt and Emma, Clare and Dean.

You all give me such hope.

Contents

Introduction

The future promise of any nation can be directly measured by the present prospects of its youth. **John F. Kennedy**

I have always loved adolescents – their enthusiasm, their quirky humour and their insightfulness. Over the years , as a teacher, I watched many of them struggle with the three big questions: Am I normal? Do I belong? Will I make it? However, in the last few years I have noticed more and more of them are asking: Will humankind make it?

This book is being written during the 2020 COVID-19 pandemic – a time of tremendous global unrest. Many people have been disturbed by the mental health crisis that has emerged, particularly amongst young people. It is assumed this has come about because of the social disruption and chaos caused by the pandemic. However, I know this is not true. For many years, I watched the number of students in my classes struggling with anxiety and depression grow. I have followed the disturbing statistics that show that the mental health of young people in Australia – considered to be one of the most advanced countries in the world – has been deteriorating for a number of years. It has become a matter of deep concern to me.

Mental health is usually discussed in terms of a medical model. When a problem arises it is assumed the young person who has a condition can be diagnosed and treated by a professional, and the answer to the growing problem is an increase in government funding to train more professionals or run more prevention programs in schools and communities.

This book questions that assumption. John Marsden, well-known author of young adult fiction and principal of two progressive schools, stated in his book *The Art of Growing Up*:

> ...if I were to generalise about adolescents in Australia in the 21st-century I would say they are highly aware. They are idealistic and passionate, particularly about human suffering and environmental issues and they are eager to see change.[1]

Could it be that the cause for the growing despair of young people lies within the way our society is functioning?

This book looks at the old story that drives our society and then presents a new story waiting to be told – an optimistic story that brings hope. The story presents the vision of a society that cares about the wellbeing of all members of society and the environment they live in. Such a society is symbolised by the majestic tree captured on the cover of this book, by artist Kaylie Rogers. Trees provide a sense of safety and comfort to those who shelter in and beneath them. However, just as a tree needs water to flourish, members of a society need nourishment to sustain their ability to be truly human and nourish one another.

This book explores the energy of the heart, which is expressed through its own language: hope, empathy, action, relationships and trust.

Throughout the book, we hear the voice of a talented young poet and writer; 17-year-old school student Ciara Symons. Through poems and writing, Ciara gives us her perspective about being a young person in the 21st century and shares her observations regarding the society we have created, as well as her thoughts about how we could do better in the future.

The reader will be invited to be part of **The Heart's Language Project** to make a contribution to creating a world where our young people cannot only survive but thrive.

Part I
Chapter 1:
The old story

There can be no keener revelation of a society's soul than the way in which it treats its children. **Nelson Mandela**

For centuries, the Maasai tribes have been known as some of the most fearsome hunters in Africa. Many are surprised to learn that the traditional greeting passed between the Maasai warriors is 'Kasserian ingera', which means, 'How are the children?' This is because they have always known that the wellbeing of a society and the wellbeing of its children are inextricably linked.

In January 2020, a biological mutation of a microscopic crown of spikes began its sweep across the globe, attacking everybody in its path regardless of nationality or ethnicity, faction or faith. The pandemic has killed hundreds of thousands, lacerated families, pulverised dreams and brought nations and their economies to their knees. Many young people are left struggling with mental health issues, and doctors have warned it is likely there will be an increase in youth suicide.[2] This is distressing but, sadly, not surprising. It is the extension of a trend that has been underway for a number of years.

In 2017, a joint report by Mission Australia – a national Christian charity – and the Black Dog Institute – a not-for-profit facility for mood disorders – found that nearly one in four Australian teenagers met the criteria for having a 'probable mental illness'.[3] This statistic backs up what most people interacting with teenagers already know from experience. Many secondary school principals have told me that anxiety is sometimes more of a hurdle than intelligence, motivation or social background for students to fulfil their potential at school. In April 2019, there were reports that even primary school principals were seeing increased mental health issues in their schools.[4] A survey of community members, conducted by the Australian Research Alliance for Children and Youth (ARACY) and the BUPA Health Foundation, found that most respondents said they believed the mental health of young people in Australia today is worse than when they were young.[5]

In September 2019, the Australian Bureau of Statistics released causes of death data from the previous year, including national suicide. Orygen, the National Centre of Excellence in Youth Mental Health, after assessing the data, stated that the rate of young Australians dying by suicide continues to increase.[6] Money and social status are no protection. In 2019, the Australian Productivity Commission, a taskforce of the Australian Government, put forward its findings regarding the effect of mental health on economic participation and productivity in Australia. While you cannot put a price on mental health, the report found that mental illness and suicide have a dramatic impact on the economy, costing the Australian society an estimated $500 million per day.[7]

The anxiety epidemic

In 2008, Martin Seligman, world-renowned United States psychologist and guru in the field of 'positive psychology', worked with the prestigious Melbourne private school Geelong Grammar. The school spent $16 million on a wellness facility to support its students because of 'the high prevalence of depression among young people worldwide'.[8] John Marsden, speaking about his experience as a school principal, has said:

> In recent years we have seen a staggering growth in the levels of anxiety among children and parents. This impacts us every day, and sometimes I feel we run ourselves ragged trying to support anxious children and teenagers, and pacify panicking parents. It's as though we had the epidemic of eating disorders, then the epidemic of self-harming, and now, although those other behaviours are still with us, we have the phenomenon of panic attacks.[9]

On the ABC program *Q&A* in September 2019, a nurse, who had set up a health clinic in a primary school, asked the panel what was to be done about what she called the 'anxiety epidemic'. She asked this question because instead of dealing with bumped heads and bruises, as expected, she found most of her time was taken up with children struggling with anxiety. A young mother on the panel reinforced her concerns saying she was shocked to see notices about how to deal with children suffering from anxiety, which had appeared at her daughter's childcare centre. Trying to explain the reasons for this situation, the panellists suggested it could be because of exhausted parents, poor nutrition or insufficient sleep, but, in reality, nobody had an answer.[10]

So, why do so many young people in our society struggle? The mental health of young people is usually discussed in terms of a medical model because it is seen as an illness that can be diagnosed and treated by trained professionals or prevented by programs in schools and communities. The solution to the problem is usually seen as increased government funding in both these areas. There have been a number of helplines and services established in the community and a plethora of programs introduced in schools, but, as the years have passed, the problem seems only to have grown worse.

Of course, trained professionals, specialised services and preventative programs are all essential to supporting young people struggling with mental health issues, but have we asked the right questions? If we do not find out the core reason for the declining mental health of our young people, increasing services and programs may be like putting water into a bucket with holes in the bottom. What if it is a symptom of a much larger problem? What if, at its core, it is about the society we have created and what we tell our young people about what makes life worth living? If we found that a fish was sick because it was swimming in a tank with toxic water, treating the fish for the illness and putting it back into the tank would not make much sense.

The 2017 Royal Commission into Institutional Responses to Child Sexual Abuse shone a light on the institutions that had turned a blind eye to the sexual abuse of young people in their care. It highlighted a shocking abdication of the duty of care by those in positions of responsibility. However, it was also an indication of a bigger problem that spans not just the church system but the whole of society. In an abandonment of our responsibility to the young, we had stopped paying attention to the insidious ways our broader society operates. The story that has been guiding contemporary society in Australia holds a greater clue.

Our belief system

Humans are storied beings, and overarching narratives allow us to make sense of who we are and the world in which we live. They are not a set of facts but, rather, a set of beliefs that give meaning and are based on fundamental assumptions about human nature. These assumptions range from the Christian belief of Original Sin, which states we are born broken and can only be saved through an intervention from God, or the more optimistic view of French philosopher Rousseau, which asserts that we are born good and our fundamental nature is to be concerned with the welfare of others.

There are a number of stories we Australians have told ourselves. The story we love to tell on our national days – Australia Day and Anzac Day – is that Australia is all about a 'fair go for all', 'mateship', 'equality'; that we, as a nation, are a good bunch who look out for each other. On Australia Day, whoever is our current prime minister will say the right things about the extraordinary finalists for the various awards: Young Australian, Senior Australian, Local Hero, and Australian of the Year. We will be told these people 'light the way' for us and are 'shining examples of our best selves', and we will be invited to applaud their 'generosity', 'compassion' and 'selflessness' because they have built the bridges of mutual respect that support the harmony within our society's diversity. In schools, we tell children they must respect and cooperate with others, show integrity, be honest and trustworthy, and be willing to speak up and report unethical behaviour.

However, there is another story that has been told in Australia that probably better reflects the reality we have been living in and explains why we are a country where the rich are getting richer and more and more people are becoming marginalised. This story, which has dominated our politics since the 1980s, is based on the neoliberal dogma shaped largely by Austrian economist Friedrich Hayek, who believed humans are fundamentally selfish and happiest when serving their self-interests. He believed society benefits us most when individuals have total choice because it leads to competition, innovation and individuals – as consumers – getting the best outcomes.

To Hayek, individualism and market forces drive a vibrant society, whereas government interference dulls that vibrancy and ultimately harms society. He accepted the fact that in such a society there would be inequality, but he dismissed concerns about this because it is necessary; there needs to be diversity and division of labour for a market economy to be successful.[11] He saw the point of society as being to enable people to pursue their 'individuality', and that the aim of any transaction or, indeed, interaction should be personal profit. He believed that business, as expressed in market forces, should take centre stage, and 'business decisions' should be able to be made regardless of any societal wellbeing or environmental harm. To him, such feelings as altruism and solidarity were 'primitive feelings' and products of hunter–gatherer societies who had to depend on shared food and solidarity for survival.[12] To him, untrammelled self-interest in the marketplace was both moral and modern.[13] The concept of a shared vision for the common good, and non-market relationships, based on compassion and empathy, were of little interest.

This way of thinking led to a belief in trickle-down economics, which is based on the idea that the best way to stimulate an economy is to give tax breaks and benefits for corporations, and the wealth will trickle down to everyone else and stimulate economic growth, benefiting all members of society.[14] The argument is based on the assumption that the wealthy will actually allow this to happen in a fair and equitable manner and not use this to entrench their positions of privilege.

Breakdown in trust of institutions

If you have any doubt that this story has seduced society and that the subsequent 'win at any cost' mentality has become a dominant mindset in recent times, you only have to look at two events in 2018. The first took place in the cultural sphere, in that most sacred of spaces for many Australians: the world of cricket. The captain of the Australian national cricket team has always been placed on a high pedestal, and his job has been described by some as being second only in importance to the prime minister. In March of that year, it was revealed that the Australian cricket team had, in order to win the huge prize money, resorted to cheating by tampering with the ball to gain a short-term advantage in a test match with South Africa. The nation looked on in horror as the captain shed tears of remorse on national television and was banished in disgrace. It watched the leaders of Australian cricket retreating, even though they tried to abrogate responsibility and wash their hands of the whole grubby affair.

Later in the year, another scandal, this time in the economic sphere, shook Australia's faith in its financial system. A Royal Commission into Australia's financial institutions exposed the sector's voracious thirst for self-aggrandisement and showed a system that had rotted from the inside. Money had become its purpose, and everyone from the teller to the CEO was rewarded for building profit for the organisation, even if it was at the expense of customers' best interests. Ken Henry, who was then Chairman of the Board at National Australia Bank, explained to the commission why dishonesty and unethical behaviour

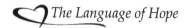

had become entrenched in the sector: 'The capitalist model is businesses have no responsibility other than to maximise profit to their shareholders.'[15]

Insidious marketing

Young people and their families are not exempt from the focus on profits over all other concerns. This can be seen in the aggressive world of marketing, which is always looking for opportunities for expansion and increased profits. This sector uses the natural curiosity and gullibility of young children and the vulnerability of adolescents to gain rich rewards.

The intrusion of marketing into the lives of children starts early. Sophisticated techniques are used to prepare young children to become brand loyal and constantly want new products. Some of the most probing and detailed knowledge of children's private lives is held by advertisers, who mine academic literature, employ psychologists and market researchers, and use focus groups to understand the fantasies, desires, fears and behaviours of children in order to exploit their developmental vulnerabilities for their own profit. For example, the Geppetto Group has studied the characteristics of children's relationships with family members and other children to make their products mirror the best of those relational feelings so as to develop compelling brand imaging. Clients of Geppetto have included Coca-Cola and McDonalds.[16]

In 1978, two Canadian social scientists, wanting to explore the effect of advertising on young children, undertook a study with a group of four and five year olds. They divided them into two groups. One group was shown no commercials while the other was shown an ad for a particular toy. The children were then offered a choice of playing with two different boys: one boy was holding the toy seen in the commercial, but the children were warned he was mean; the other little boy was not holding a toy, but the children were told he was friendly. The group not shown the commercial mainly chose the boy with no toy, while the other group mostly chose the boy in the commercial with the toy, showing how the advertisement contributed to the children choosing an inferior human connection over a superior human connection.[17]

The messaging of the marketing world heats up as children transition from childhood through the tweens (ages 8–12) through to their teenage years. At this stage, children are bombarded with limiting media stereotypes on what it is to be a girl or a boy in today's world. Of growing concern to many psychologists and doctors has been the marketing to children in a way that is explicitly sexual, such as little girls in commercials wearing makeup and toddler push-up bras, which contributes to the sexualisation of young girls. This is reinforced in the media and commercial world through magazines, television programs containing adult themes, and music videos with sexually explicit dance routines or provocative lyrics.

For years, experts have warned that this exposure can lay the foundation for eating disorders, anxiety and depression, as girls' sense of worth becomes associated with their ability to live up to the narrow concept of attractiveness presented by the marketing world. We are also warned that this lays the foundation for young boys to see girls as sexual objects, judging their value in terms of their physical attractiveness. These concerns have been highlighted in two reports: *Letting Children be Children* (2002)[18] and *Corporate Paedophilia: Sexualisation of children in Australia* (2006), both by The Australia Institute.[19]

By the time children enter adolescence – a time of heightened anxiety over looks and popularity – the seeds have been sown for them to become ideal consumers. The marketing world puts forward idealised images to make them feel inadequate and then pushes on them products that allow them to think they will become like the images they see. They are encouraged to continually worry about their appearance and about gaining the approval of others, thus creating a dangerous self-absorption that increases their chances of becoming narcissistic and anxious.

During the pandemic, lockdown parents have felt the true weight of Big Tech as they have watched their adolescents, removed from normal activities, get drawn in by video games to the extent that it has become a daily battle to get them off the screen, causing conflict in already fraught environments. Many of these games are set up to be addictive as players are seduced by the promise of rewards by completing ongoing missions or getting involved in multiplayer games with peers, which have no endings. Some of the games involve real money to unlock different levels. Many parents have reported feeling powerless to match the sophisticated techniques used by the creators of the games that keep their children hooked.

One cruel trick played by marketers has been to focus on parents, as children and adolescents do not have the resources to pay for goods themselves. In 2004, a poll of youth marketers found 73 per cent of people working in the youth industry agreed that most companies put pressure on children to pester their parents to buy things.[20] They do this even though they know it causes stress and conflict in families.

Social toxicity

As the number of relationships based on competition, self-interest and suspicion have grown, bonds based on respect, civility and trust have been weakened, and the casualties from this old story have been care, trust, decency and compassion, particularly towards the weak and vulnerable. Royal commissions have shown how children in institutions, people with disabilities and the fragile aged have been abused by the people they thought they could trust. Through the pandemic, the hardest-hit sector has been aged care. It was revealed that the sector had been under-resourced for many years. The stark image of a 95-year-old woman with ants crawling from a wound on her leg and the bandages around it crusted with blood in a COVID-19-affected Melbourne aged care facility said it all.[21] Vulnerability has come to be seen as a moral failure and a drain. Gerry Harvey, from the Harvey Norman chain, stated this bluntly and callously when he said:

> You could go out and give a million dollars to a charity tomorrow to help the homeless. You could argue that it is just wasted. They are not putting anything back into the community. It might be a callous way of putting it but what are they doing? You are helping a whole heap of no-hopers to survive for no good reason. They are just a drag on the whole community.[22]

The 'prosperity gospel' – a religious belief that states financial fortune is a sign of God's favour – has reinforced this viewpoint and is central to a number of Christian churches, some of which are attended by some of our leading politicians.[23]

You do not have to look hard to see that the tears in the social fabric are growing in many aspects of Australian life. In July 2019, the Australian public was shocked when a Jewish Year

7 student at Cheltenham Secondary College in Melbourne was filmed while being forced to kiss the shoes of a Muslim boy under threat of being swarmed by several other boys. The incident was shared on social media.[24] The incident highlighted the tensions that exist between different groups in schools. However, teachers will tell you that what happens in schools is merely a reflection of the social and political disharmony of wider society, where sexism, misogyny, racism, cyberbullying, homophobia and religious intolerance are fuelled by some media outlets, which focus on conflict, turmoil and a hostile social media environment where people attack those who think differently to themselves.

In August 2019, it was reported that the growing number of aggressive and violent incidents involving federal members of parliament in Australia has sparked a spike in referrals to national security agencies. Politicians warn that Australia's increasingly toxic political debate could lead to tragic consequences.[25] Greens senator Sarah Hanson-Young has stated, 'It is no surprise that nasty rhetoric in public debate gives individuals licence to be aggressive and threatening. It is worrying that anonymous aggression and vitriol seen online and on social media are becoming normalised.' She says that death threats and rape threats are now part of her daily life.[26]

This toxicity is ramped up by a number of media commentators. In 2019, when Scott Morrison was going to have a meeting with Jacinda Ardern – Prime Minister of New Zealand – Alan Jones, who was then a Sydney radio commentator, encouraged him to 'shove a sock down her throat'.[27]

The social problems in our society run deep. Every week, a woman is killed violently by her partner, every day about six men commit suicide, and every night 120,000 people have no place to call their home.

16

Young people are like tuning forks, picking up the vibrations of a broken society. One is reminded of Ovid's tale of Erysichthon from Greek mythology:

Erysichthon was a wealthy timber merchant. A greedy man who thought only of profit. Nothing was sacred to him. On his land was a sacred grove of Demeter's, Goddess of the harvest, growth and nourishment. She presided over the fertility of the Earth. Erysichthon looked at the grove and assessed the profit from the wood of the trees there. He ordered his men to cut them all down. However, they baulked when they came to the sacred tree, a huge oak covered with votive wreaths, each a symbol of every prayer Demeter had granted. Erysichthon was extremely angry. He took an axe and cut it down himself until all divine life that had inhabited the tree had fled. However, one of the gods put a curse on him, and an insatiable hunger consumed him. He began by eating all his stores. He then turned all his wealth into food he could consume. Still not satisfied, he consumed his wife and children. In the end, Erysichthon was left with nothing to consume but his flesh. He eats himself.[28]

Observations from yours truly, a Youth

Ciara M. Symons

This is what I've noticed: there is a pain I believe every human can feel, but not everyone can identify. It is not a stab; it is not your heart being battered. No, this one can lie dormant inside you, and then it begins to grow. When you realise it's there, it's – well – quite heavy.

It is a pain nobody talks about. It's the bottling up you were warned about. You are told that holding it in will only get worse. But ah, that's the conundrum; no-one gave you the emotional bottle opener.

It feels like a defence: a thickening of the flesh around the heart, formed from scrapes and callouses.

Let me tell you what has created these callouses.

*My **personal anxieties** are my trials. They create the narrative that is my life. I mostly haven't succeeded at overcoming these hardships. But the majority of them don't matter; the only reason they have mattered is because I believed a little too brashly that they did. I find it hard to distinguish what matters and what doesn't, and therefore it comes down to my own assessment. It is hard to balance criticism and sympathy in the analyses.*

The patriarchy

The power structure underpinning the way our society functions is the patriarchy, defined as a social system where men hold most positions of power because of the assumption that men are superior to women. One of the outcomes of this has been a profound disrespect for women.

The influence of the patriarchy on boys growing up in our society was on open display in an incident that occurred on a Melbourne tram on Saturday, 19 October, 2019. With a high level of confidence and without shame, a group of Year 10 and 11 boys from St Kevin's College – an elite Catholic all-boys school in Melbourne – were filmed in full uniform on a packed tram chanting the following lyrics on their way to an inter-school sports carnival:[29]

I wish that all the ladies

Were holes in the road

And if I were a dump truck

I'd fill them with my load

The lines come from a sexist 16-line chant that originated in the military as one of many marching songs detailing explicit and degrading sexual acts men want to perform on women. A week later, Year 12 boys from the same school chanted a similar verse at an end-of-year pub crawl in Richmond.[30]

What happened after these events proved interesting. The principal stated he was shocked and said the school would be working hard to educate the boys about respect for women.[31] Some students stated, however, that a 'hyper-masculine, totally misogynistic culture pervaded all levels at St Kevin's'[32], and a former student expressed that the boys had learned and practised the chant on a school camp in Year 8, and that there had been teachers in the vicinity, and they did not raise any objections.[33]

In the middle of this commentary, another student from the school reflected on his Facebook page that the misogynistic actions of the students were not because of the culture at the school but were instead 'the fault of our wider society'.[34] This was backed up by journalist Emma Jane, who observed, 'There's a reason St Kevin's College boys started a sexist chant: society is geared against women... any messaging about respect within formal sensitisation programs undertaken by the school would take place in a society which discriminates against and disadvantages girls and women on almost every significant measure, so it is little wonder there is a disconnect for the boys.'[35]

The history of patriarchy

In trying to understand the power of patriarchy, David Leser, in his book *Women, men & the whole damn thing*, sets out to explore its historical background and insidious influence in our present society. Leser describes himself as a 'straight, middle-class male who has breathed the untroubled air of privilege' all his life.[36] He says he does not claim to 'speak for women' but rather sees his book as 'an attempt to investigate, as a writer and a man, how murderous male hatred and disrespect rages across the world against billions of women and girls, of all colours, creeds, classes and ages.'[37]

He found its seeds in ancient Western philosophical and religious writings as far back as Aristotle; a towering figure of ancient Greek philosophy, who stated, 'The female is female by virtue of a certain lack of qualities. We should regard women's nature as suffering from natural defectiveness.'[38]

In the story of creation in the Christian Bible, we are told that God fashioned Eve from the rib of Adam and said, 'She shall be called woman because she was taken out of man.' It then instructs women that the desire of a wife 'shall be for your husband and he shall rule over you'.[39]

Early Christian fathers were quite open in viewing their belief in females' inferiority. Tertullian, the second-century Latin Christian author – regarded as the founder of Western theology – described the vagina as a 'temple built over a sewer' and the 'Devil's gateway'.[40] Influential Christian philosopher Thomas Aquinas declared women to be 'defective and misbegotten'.[41] In his book, Leser cites Simone de Beauvoir who, in her landmark history of feminism *The Second Sex*, quotes St Augustine, one of the most influential figures in Christianity, as saying a woman is a 'beast who is neither firm nor stable'.[42]

Outcomes of patriarchy

The scale of violence against women in the modern world demonstrates that patriarchy still has a firm grip. The United Nations states that violence against women is a violation of human rights as it negatively impacts on both the physical and mental wellbeing of women and girls across the world.[43]

The Australian Women Donors Network in Melbourne estimates that there are four million women and girls bought and sold worldwide, forced into prostitution, slavery or marriage.[44] WHO estimates that up to 130 million women and girls worldwide have been subjected to total or partial removal of their clitorises.[45] Other abuses of women include bride and widow burning, forced marriage and female foeticide (i.e., the abortion of the female foetus outside of legal methods).[46] In Australian women aged 15–44, intimate partner violence is the leading contributor to death and disability.[47]

One of the most glaring areas of injustice against women is inequality in the workplace. The Women Donors Network has demonstrated that throughout the world, women work 66 per cent of the world's working hours, yet earn only 10 per cent of the world's income.[48] In Australia, women earn less than men for doing the same or comparable work.[49] The gender pay gap is the difference between women and men's average weekly full-time equivalent earnings, expressed as a percentage of men's earnings. Using the Australian Bureau of Statistics' Average Weekly Full-Time Earnings data, the national gender pay gap is currently 17.1 per cent and has hovered between 15 and 18 per cent for the past two decades.[50] Even though 57 per cent of university graduates are women, they represent less than 10 per cent of ASX board seats, and more than half of ASX 500 companies have no female executives and only 12 have a female CEO.[51] Women in Australia are two and a half times more likely to live in poverty in their old age than men.[52]

It has been shown that even being in a position of power does not protect a woman from being confronted by misogyny. When Julia Gillard became the first female prime minister of Australia, she was attacked relentlessly. One male politician labelled her as being 'deliberately barren' and the then Opposition Leader Tony Abbott stood in front of a placard screaming 'BITCH' and 'DITCH THE WITCH' while speaking to an anti-carbon tax rally in 2011.[53] Alan Jones suggested she be placed in a 'chaff bag' and taken out to sea and also suggested that her beloved father had died of shame because she was a liar.[54]

One of the most globally shocking incidents of violence against a woman took place in India in 2012. At 9.30pm on 16 December, a 23-year-old medical student, Jyoti Singh, boarded a bus in the south of Delhi with her male friend Awindra Pandey. They were met on the bus by six drunken men on a 'joyride' demanding to know why a woman was out so late with someone who was neither her husband nor her brother. An argument ensued, and Pandey was beaten, gagged and knocked unconscious. Singh was dragged to the back of the bus, gang-raped, penetrated with a rusty iron rod, and disembowelled. Along with Pandey, Jyoti's body was dumped half-naked from the moving bus and found at about 11pm by a passer-by.[55] When the news broke of this appalling crime, India erupted into the largest, most sustained protest against gender-based violence ever seen in the country and surrounding countries.

Male conditioning

Leslee Udwin, a renowned filmmaker, was horrified and made the film *India's Daughter* about the event.[56] She believed the enormous wave of protest would be the end of violence against women, but it soon became apparent that violence against women continued. She became curious about the type of men who had committed the crime and what motivated them, so she asked permission to interview them. After thirty-one hours of being with the men, she stated:

> It would have been easier to process this heinous crime if they had been deranged monsters, rotten apples in the barrel. However, this could not be further from the truth. It is the barrel that is rotten, and the barrel rots the apples.[57]

She came to see that the rapists were ordinary men. She discovered that it was their conditioning that caused them, just like many men around the world, to be programmed from the earliest age to view females with disdain and to assume a certain type of masculinity.[58]

A number of men have come forward to articulate how that conditioning occurs. One of these, Tony Porter – co-founder of A Call To Men – in a TED Talk speaks about what he was taught when he was growing up in New York. He says he was taught that real men are tough, strong and courageous and do not display emotion other than anger. He was also taught that men are superior and women are their property.[59] In another TED Talk – 'Why I'm done trying to be "man enough"' – actor Justin Baldoni explains how he was told when he was growing up that if one wanted to be accepted by other boys, one had to reject any qualities that could be considered feminine because women were to be looked down upon because they are weak. He believes that this is what is being subconsciously communicated to hundreds of millions of young boys all over the world, just as it was to him.[60]

Carl Jung, the Swiss psychoanalyst renowned for his theory of the collective unconscious, stated that men and women have within them the ability to access both female and male qualities. He called the feminine within man *the anima*, which, when activated, allows men to experience tenderness, compassion, vulnerability, relatedness, creativity, imagination and intuition.[61] In our culture, a rigid script of masculinity has encouraged men to renounce their feminine qualities and embrace aggression and anger as markers of real manhood.

Steve Biddulph, a well-known psychologist who has worked with men and boys in hundreds of seminars, says this has left men becoming severed from their emotions in a way that leaves them feeling vulnerable and confused. He said that he himself, when he was young, was like many boys who did not know how 'to do male'. He says to deal with this they 'clamped on a mask' every morning, hoping that it would last until night and 'no-one would notice'.[62]

Men being unable to express their vulnerability has had tragic consequences for society. One such consequence is one of the most intractable problems in our society – domestic violence. For many years, it was assumed that men are violent just to show they have power and control over a woman. However, researcher Jess Hill, having looked through all the research on the topic, conducted dozens of interviews with abusive men and consulted with international experts, found that many abusers actually harbour a deep desire for intimacy and belonging and feel vulnerable when they do not get what they want from a relationship. However, rather than acknowledging those feelings, they feel ashamed and humiliated by their own perceived weakness, so they attack their partners to try to show they are strong and in control.[63]

Another tragic consequence of men being unable to get in touch with their vulnerability is developing a deep sense of despair, to the point where they want to take their own life. Research from Beyond Blue and Movember has shown that suicide is the leading cause of death for men under the age of 45, and men are three times more likely than women to take their own life.[64] As radical black feminist Bell Hooks has said:

> The first act of violence that patriarchy demands of males is not violence toward women. Instead patriarchy demands of all males that they engage in acts of psychic self-mutilation, that they kill off the emotional parts of themselves.[65]

Time for a reset

This is the society we have wrapped around our young people. A society where the driving forces are greed and power, and profit is more important than people. A society where trust in institutions and each other has diminished, and bitterness and hate are on the increase. At its base is a power system that diminishes both men and women. The increase in social problems, the deterioration in mental health and the decline in the 'ethic of care' are testament to a society that has lost its way. It is time for a reset.

Chapter 2:
A new story

I believe, with Ghandi, that we need to take an imaginative leap forward toward fresh and generous idealism for the sake of all humanity.
Mairead Corrigan Maguire

Geoff Gallop, ex-Premier of WA, stated in July 2019, on the national television program *Q&A*:

> Young people at the moment are the miners' canaries of our society. They're picking up the real issues that we have deep down in the way we conduct our social relationships, the way we organise our society, the priorities we give. They can't see the hope. And I think we have a responsibility in politics to recognise that factor and to build a better society ... young people are telling us something and we should be listening.[66]

The Chinese word for crisis is made up of two characters: danger and opportunity. Both have been apparent during the COVID-19 crisis. Danger has revealed itself as people have lost loved ones or experienced stressful financial circumstances. Domestic violence has increased, and many are struggling with mental health issues. However, opportunity has presented itself in the discussions that are taking place about Australia's future.

Two different views have emerged. Some people, especially those whose efforts are rewarded by the powerful political and economic systems of the old story, feel that everything should just return to 'normal'. However, others believe that going back to the status quo will mean the continuation of the inequity and greed that characterised the world before the pandemic. Having glimpsed a world of shared humanity – a world where politicians work together cooperatively for the common good, and a world where our government supports the vulnerable during the crisis – they believe a better society can be created. This is captured in the words of Indian writer Arundhati Roy:

> Whatever it is, coronavirus has made the mighty kneel and brought the world to a halt like nothing else could. Our minds are still racing back and forth, longing for a return to 'normality', trying to stitch our future to our past and refusing to acknowledge the rupture. But the rupture exists. And in the midst of this terrible despair, it offers us a chance to rethink the doomsday machine we have built for ourselves. Nothing could be worse than a return to normality.[67]

Social commentators, such as Chilean economist Manfred Max-Neef, have long been telling us that the old story has not served us well. It has failed because the satisfaction promised by consumerism is false, involving an endless round of identity construction through fashion and the constant messaging that we must 'keep up'. It is false because it does not meet people's real needs, which are self-worth, connection, understanding, participation, creation, identity and freedom.[68]

Other social researchers have come to a similar conclusion. For over 25 years, American psychologist Tim Kasser carried out many studies to explore the link between what people value and their sense of happiness and wellbeing. He established an

Aspiration Index, which focuses on two sets of aspirations. The first are extrinsic motives, which describe the things we do not do because they bring enjoyment but because we get something in return, such as money, admiration or status. The second set are intrinsic motives; things done for their value in themselves because they bring joy to our life rather than material reward. For example, connecting with friends, doing good things for others, or taking action to make the world a better place. He created a mechanism by which people could self-report on their state of mind, be it a sense of wellbeing or a level of anxiety and depression. In all the studies, he found that people who achieved their extrinsic goals did not experience any increase in day-to-day happiness, but those who spent time following their intrinsic goals became significantly happier and less depressed and anxious. He concluded that this could be because the system has conditioned people to be continually anxious because they feel they always need more than they already have.[69]

An optimistic view of human nature

Our young people are crying out for a new story; a story that enhances the human spirit, a story that takes their future seriously. They want a story that encourages people to care for each other and the planet by finding brave and creative ideas to address the challenges the world faces and that gives hope. There are thousands eager to tell that story, and it is waiting in the wings to become the story that guides our society.

So, what is this new story?

In contrast to the bleak, pessimistic view of the old story, which sees human life as nasty and brutish with greed overriding all other instincts, the new story believes that, while humans are obviously capable of violence and selfishness, the basic instinct of most humans tends toward kindness. There is a lot of evidence to support this point of view.

In the face of the vicious pandemic, when it could be easy for fear and selfishness to rule, across the world, people have reached out to help each other. For example:

- In Bangalore, India, one little restaurant, called Desi Masala, feeds more than 10,000 vulnerable people every day, just like thousands of other volunteers who help cook fresh, healthy food for frontline workers and those in need.
- After decades of fighting each other, rival gangs around Cape Town agreed on an unprecedented truce and work together to bring food to struggling households in their communities.
- Scientists across the globe have collaborated to find a vaccine against COVID-19, and world leaders have pledged €7.4 billion to help ensure the vaccine is distributed in poorer countries.
- In Naples, Italy, people leave 'solidarity baskets' out for those who are struggling, with a note that reads: 'Put in, if you can. Take out, if you can't.'
- Portugal has given all refugees and migrants with pending applications full citizenship during the crisis, granting them access to free health care, welfare benefits, bank accounts and rental contracts.[70]

During the pandemic, Australians have also reached out to look after each other, and there have been countless acts of kindness reported throughout the country. It is similar to the behaviour shown earlier in 2020 when, during a catastrophic bushfire season, thousands of Australians stepped up to help when they saw the images and heard the stories of their fellow citizens suffering. Money, goods and offers of help flowed in from every sector of the community. People sewed or knitted garments for wounded wildlife and opened up their homes to welcome fire refugees. Professional tennis players organised a Rally for Relief, which raised millions of dollars for the appeal.

Some of the most generous groups during this time were those often discriminated against because of their ethnicity or belief system. For example, a small refugee community, the Hazaras in Victoria, raised a large amount of money to help their 'brothers and sisters', while volunteers from Sydney's Sikh community transported semi-trailer loads of water and other goods and helped farmers fix their fences. The Islamic community raised large amounts of money and travelled long distances to take supplies to fire-affected areas. Many affected people showed extreme gratitude for the kindness of strangers.

In January 2017, the people of Melbourne showed the same spirit by staying with the injured when a reckless driver killed six people and injured thirty others in the CBD. The incident caused one paramedic to say, 'Wherever I looked and there was someone injured, they weren't on their own. In a strange way, it was an awesome experience to see so many people step up and care for each other.'[71]

There is scientific evidence to support this optimistic view. A significant study, reported in *Scientific American* in 2012, by a diverse group of researchers from Harvard and Yale, wanted to explore the question: Is the automatic impulse of people, i.e., their first instinct, to act selfishly or cooperatively? The researchers included a developmental psychologist, with a background in evolutionary game theory, a moral philosopher-turned-psychologist, and a biologist-cum-mathematician. They wanted to analyse human nature, not through a philosopher's kaleidoscope or the voice of economic theorists, but through the clear lens of science. The experimenters first examined potential links between processing speed, selfishness and cooperation by using two experimental paradigms (the 'prisoner's dilemma' and a 'public goods game'). They carried out five studies, with 834 participants gathered from both undergraduate campuses and a nationwide sample.

Each paradigm consisted of group-based financial decision-making tasks and required participants to choose between acting selfishly – opting to maximise individual benefits at the cost of the group – or cooperatively, opting to maximise group benefits at the cost of the individual. It explored the difference between two forms of decision-making: intuition and reflection. Intuition is automatic and effortless and leads to actions that occur without insight into the reasons behind them. Reflection, on the other hand, is all about conscious thought, which weighs the costs and benefits of likely outcomes and rationally decided on courses of action. Using that dual-process framework, they wanted to boil the complexities of basic human nature down to a simple question: which behaviour – selfishness or cooperation – is intuitive and which is the product of rational reflection? In other words, do humans cooperate when they overcome their intuitive selfishness with rational self-control, or do they act selfishly when they override their intuitive cooperative impulses with rational self-interest?

They carried out many other experiments with different groups. Although no single set of studies can provide a definitive answer, the results were striking. In every study, faster, more intuitive decisions were associated with higher levels of cooperation, whereas slower, more reflective decisions were associated with higher levels of selfishness. These results suggested that the first impulse of humans is to cooperate.[72]

Holistic thinking

Recent findings in neuroscience have shown that human beings are hardwired to connect, help and cooperate with others, and they flourish emotionally and physically when they do so. They have also shown that when acts involving generosity, selflessness and compassion are undertaken, they activate reward centres in the brain.[73]

A new story recognises that wellbeing is not only tied to material or individual fulfilment but includes collective, spiritual and ecological dimensions. Expressions used in other cultures capture this concept. In South Africa, the word 'ubuntu' means 'I am because you are'. In South America, the Indigenous and Andean peoples' expression 'buen vivir' means 'living well', recognising that the individual is always inherently part of the community. The North Alaskan word 'nuka' expresses the need for people to reconnect with their community and the importance of physical, mental, emotional and spiritual wellness.

This type of thinking links in with a matriarchal consciousness that focuses on the interconnectedness of life. It is typified by right brain, intuitional and holistic thinking, which embraces our relationship to the whole and the cyclical renewal of things, whereas the patriarchal consciousness is typified by a more left-brain, rational, analytic and linear thinking, where the individual is perceived as separate from others and from nature. The patriarchal consciousness has fostered the illusion that humans can conquer and control the natural world with impunity, without regard for the ecological interdependence of all life forms. This way of thinking has been shattered by the COVID-19 crisis as the fragility of the world we have created is revealed.

The human race has been challenged to relearn the wisdom Indigenous communities have always known: humans are part of the complex web of relationships, and the survival of the species depends on respecting the boundaries of what contributes to the health of that web. The message is clear: *we need to look after nature so that nature looks after us.*

The new story encourages a shift in the attitudes of men to move away from the current broken way of thinking about masculinity so that they can embrace a healthier masculinity where being sensitive or emotionally engaged is not seen as a weakness but part of being a fully rounded adult human.

Part of reclaiming a healthy masculinity means men supporting equal rights for women so that both sexes can move forward with common values and respect. In September 2018, New Zealand Prime Minister Jacinda Ardern told the United Nations: 'Me Too must become We Too [because] we are all in this together.'[74] The Bahá'í writings state: 'The world of humanity is possessed of two wings, the male and the female. So long as these two wings are not equivalent in strength, the bird will not fly.'[75]

There are men already taking action to make equal rights a reality. For example: British actor Benedict Cumberbatch refuses to take roles if his female co-stars are paid less; Jakson Elfring, a young diesel mechanic from rural Victoria, published a four-and-a-half-minute video on Facebook in July 2018 decrying Australia's culture of violence towards women; and Ed Vere's latest picture book for three to seven year olds, *How to be a Lion*, employs the maxim 'you don't have to roar to be heard' because he believes 'compassion, respect and empathy need to be taught at an early foundational age'.[76]

Neuroscientists say that the optimal time is in the early years, while the brain is still forming neural pathways and before toxic attitudes have a chance to solidify. Leslee Udwin has taken up the challenge, and her international Think Equal initiative aims to transform mindsets through social and emotional learning in three- to six-year-old boys and girls in schools. The program teaches critical thinking, self-regulation, collaboration and appreciation and lays the foundation for emotional intelligence.[77]

The essence of the new story is the realisation that all humans share this planet, and we must learn to coexist. The challenges that face the world today face the entire planet. There are no national boundaries for environmental degradation and climate protection. The wellbeing of the planet and any future we may have is dependent on our innate human nature – our natural affinity for goodness, compassion and caring for others. We must learn that humanity is one big family. We are all brothers and sisters: physically, mentally and emotionally.

Observations from yours truly, a Youth

Ciara M. Symons

*We have made our lives more complicated. The oppressive ideals we are attempting to unravel are so entwined in our **culture**. Tradition is now okay in every instance. We are so strangely sentimental for tradition. But ethics – our basic principles – have developed since we started these traditions. Our philosophies have grown. We have not grown up with them. It is time to sever these traditions. But these destructive acts are so old, they have each turned into Gordian knots. And our swords – our words – are not as sharp as we initially thought. No, we cannot just bludgeon and batter away at these contorted ropes. We must pick away at them – with finesse and patience – until the knots are just frayed pieces of string, ready to be crafted into better and brighter traditions.*

Chapter 3: The new story – the revitalised local

We belong in a bundle of life. We say a person is a person through other persons. It is not I think therefore I am. It says rather: I am human because I belong, I participate, and I share. **Desmond Tutu**

A t the heart of the new story is revitalised local economies and communities because many people have come to realise that they are the key to restoring wellbeing, happiness, democracy and ecological health around the world. The dominance of globalisation and the rise of large corporations have eroded communities. One of the results has been the loss of livelihoods as big businesses displace local businesses. For example, the giant online marketer Amazon employs about 14 people for every $10 million in retail sales, while small shops employ 47 people for the same amount of sales. Another result has been environmental breakdown. The global economy has intensified the ecological consequences of industrialisation. Corporate agribusinesses poison topsoil and let it wash out to sea. The timber, oil and mining industries clear-cut millions of acres of irreplaceable forest each year. Pollution is destroying ecosystems worldwide, and species extinction is accelerating rapidly.[78]

Australian social researcher Hugh Mackay, in discussions with a wide range of people regarding their perceived quality of life, found 'loss of community' to be one of the most common concerns among contemporary Australians.[79] That concern is expressed as a regret that local neighbourhoods are not functioning as well as they once did. One of the silver linings of the pandemic has been a growth in community spirit as people were sustained by both giving and receiving help from those in their local communities. There was a collective understanding that, even though their lives mattered, so did the lives of those in their community.

Communities provide abundant opportunities for connection, be it looking after neighbours, sharing meals, playing sport together, creating together, learning together and sharing common interests. They fulfil one of the most intrinsic of human desires – to belong – and the strength of a community can make the difference between life and death. In his book *Heat Wave*, sociologist Eric Klinenberg describes his study of two adjacent neighbourhoods with similar demographics during a severe heatwave, which killed more than 700 residents in Chicago in 1995. He found one community had a death rate six times higher than the other, largely because people lacked social connections and died behind closed doors.[80] A similar situation occurred during a heatwave in Europe in 2003, where 70,000 lonely Europeans died in big cities, even though countries like France boasted strong health systems.

In communities, bridges can be built across age and socioeconomic and cultural backgrounds, so that shared experiences become the threads that weave the fabric of the community. People can become part of an identity larger than themselves, drawn out of a cocoon of self-absorption, to a place where they do not ask 'what is in this for me?' but rather, 'what is in this for us?' Thick networks can be formed, which lead to shared projects where people contribute their skills in different ways. Projects can be community shops, food assemblies (communities buying fresh food directly from local producers), community choirs, free universities (in which people exchange knowledge and skills in social spaces) and time banking (where neighbours give their time to give practical help and support to others). Other projects could be transition towns (where residents try to create more sustainable economies), potluck lunch clubs (in which everyone brings a homemade dish to share), local currencies and men's sheds (in which older men swap skills and escape from loneliness).

Rotterdam is a good example of what happens when these thick networks are formed. In response to the closure of local libraries in 2011, a group of residents created a reading room from an old Turkish bathhouse. The project began with a festival of plays, films and discussions, then became permanently embedded. It became a meeting place where people could talk, read and learn new skills and soon began, with some help from the council, to spawn restaurants, workshops, care cooperatives, green projects, cultural hubs and craft collectives. These projects inspired other people to start their own, and it is estimated that there are now 1,300 civic projects in the city. Deep cooperation and community building now feel entirely normal there.

In Todmorden, West Yorkshire, England, the Incredible Edible Villages venture began as a guerrilla planting scheme where fruit and vegetables were grown in public spaces and unused corners. The venture revitalised the local community, leading to the generation of start-ups, the creation of jobs and the establishment of training programs.[81]

Governments can provide hardware to communities through the provision of resources and infrastructure, but the software – the social capital of a community – is its local relationships and connections. Plans for community made by government departments can be like beautiful, well-crafted cars that have no fuel. The enthusiasm and commitment of the community members is the fuel needed to bring the plans to life.

Building community

Building strong communities takes time and effort. There have been many different models put forward for effective community development, but one of the most interesting and effective is the Asset-Based Community Development (ABCD) approach proposed by two American professors – John L. McKnight and John P. Kretzmann – at the Institute for Policy Research at Northwestern University in Evanston, Illinois, in 1993.[82] This approach is a set of principles that states that the most effective way to strengthen sustainable communities is to start by focusing on what is *strong* in a community rather than what is *wrong*. This empowers the community to take a grassroots approach to energise and utilise what they already possess so as to achieve common goals. This approach sees the strengths of the community as being the skills and knowledge of the individuals in the community, the associational power of the local voluntary groups as well as businesses and government institutions, the local economy and the physical world, both natural and constructed. It is based on the belief that strong communities are the ones that have moved past waiting for people and resources outside the community to help fix problems, and have come to a place where they can come up with their solutions based on their own strengths.

This approach was a reaction to the usual top-down approach, often used by governmental departments in the areas of public health, education, human services and public administration. When faced with the task of improving outcomes for individuals and groups in a community, these bodies often begin by focusing on the areas of social weakness, such as unemployment, family breakdown and substance abuse. They then develop a needs analysis and follow this up with an action plan, which involves engaging experts to provide programs and services so that community members become clients and customers, and, as programs and services target particular groups, they work in isolation, leading to the formation of silos. The existing strengths in communities are often ignored, so communities come to believe that the only solution to the challenges they face must come from outside.

ABCD has a generous and optimistic view of humanity and believes that every community has strengths, and that all members of the community have something to offer, so it invites all to be involved. It focuses on listening to people because it believes the key to engagement is trust, and things move at the speed of trust. It believes that people contribute when they are working on what matters to them, so it sets up mechanisms for people to articulate what they care about, focusing on collaboration rather than competition, and it aims to develop mindsets where the focus is on the common good rather than the interest of particular individuals. It seeks to inform, consult and engage with community members so that they co-produce and co-design what happens in their communities.

It aims to widen the circle of people motivated to take action, and it seeks to change the usual pattern in a community, where a small group of people drive all the initiatives, and the rest look on. It does not assume things always need to be done the same way, and it imagines new and creative ways of achieving outcomes by providing a wide range of opportunities, because it recognises that people want to be involved at many different levels; for example, rallying around a particular issue, turning up for work parties, organising a particular event, or just getting involved in events for social contact.

It allows communities to imagine their future together and believes that communities grow in confidence by asking three questions:

1. What can this community do for itself?
2. What does this community need support for?
3. What can this community not do for itself?

It believes that if a community can answer these questions, it develops a sense of pride and the capacity to forge its own destiny, engaging with governments and outside agencies on their own terms. The ABCD approach can be summed up in the following words by Lao Tzu:

Go to the people.

Live with them.

Learn from them.

Love them.

Start with what they know.

Build with what they have.

But with the best leaders,

When the work is done,

The task accomplished,

The people will say,

'We have done this ourselves.'[83]

Chapter 4: The new story – defining issues

The COVID-19 pandemic has highlighted a number of defining issues, which must be part of the new story.

Respect for science and climate change

One of the key lessons of the pandemic has been the importance of listening to scientific expertise. Scientists have been warning about the inevitability of a pandemic for years because of a dramatic rise in the world's population, the growth of densely populated cities, greatly expanded and faster modes of transport, the unprecedented growth of the world's livestock population and a globally interconnected economy with long supply chains. The Australian Government took these warnings seriously and showed it was prepared to act. Health experts have appeared with politicians at daily briefings during the crisis. Countries that fail to listen to the experts have been ill-prepared.

For years, scientists have been warning about another danger hovering over our society – climate change. In September 2019, thousands of Australian school students took to the streets, joining millions of other young people around the world in climate strikes. They proclaimed:

> We are school students from cities and towns across Australia. Most of us have never met in person before but are united by our concern about our planet. We are striking from school to tell our politicians to take our futures seriously and treat climate change for what it is – a crisis.[84]

Greta Thunberg, who had initiated the worldwide action, was asked to speak to the United Nations Climate Change Summit held at that time. Her bold words shook the world:

> This is all wrong. I shouldn't be up here. I should be back in school on the other side of the ocean. Yet you all come to us young people for hope. How dare you! You have stolen my dreams and my childhood with your empty words. For more than 30 years, the science has been crystal clear. You are failing us. But the young people are starting to understand your betrayal. The eyes of all future generations are upon you. And if you choose to fail us, I say: We will never forgive you. We will not let you get away with this. Right here, right now is where we draw the line. The world is waking up. And change is coming, whether you like it or not. Thank you.[85]

In February 2020, thousands of frustrated Australian citizens joined together in a two-day National Climate Emergency Summit (NCE Summit) in Melbourne, and, at the end of this, a number of influential Australians put forward the following declaration:[86]

Australia's 2019–20 megafires are a harbinger of life and death on a hotter Earth. The climate is already dangerous – in Australia and the Antarctic, in Asia and the Pacific – right around the world. The Earth is unacceptably too hot now.

The impacts of climate disruption are more severe than previously projected. At 1.5°C warming relative to pre-industrial levels, now likely only a decade away, the Great Barrier Reef will be lost, sea levels will be heading for a rise of many metres, and tipping points will be at hand for Greenland, and for the Amazon and other carbon stores.

The current Paris Agreement emission reduction commitments, if implemented, are a path to 3.5°C warming by 2100, possibly earlier. This could increase to 4–5°C when long-term climate-system feedbacks are considered. National security analysts warn that 3°C may result in "outright social chaos", and 4°C is considered incompatible with the maintenance of human civilisation.

Leading scientists warn of a "Hot House Earth" scenario, a planetary threshold that may exist at a temperature rise as low as 2°C, in which further warming becomes self-sustaining. The challenge now is to return to a safe climate by cooling the Earth whilst avoiding tipping points which may initiate further warming.

This requires an emergency response, where climate is a primary concern of leadership at all levels.

In late 2019 and early 2020, a catastrophic fire event, which burned eight million hectares of land, killed millions of native animals and displaced whole communities, gave the Australian public a glimpse of how climate change could impact our world.

45

They looked on in horror at the images on their television screens – skies turning pitch-black or blood-red in the middle of the day, terrified holidaymakers huddling on beaches to shelter from the flames, tornadoes of fire tossing enormous trucks into the air and fire fronts too big for volunteers to fight. They looked to the federal government and found it had been asleep at the wheel. A request for a meeting with the Prime Minister by 24 concerned ex-fire chiefs had been turned down,[87] and a National Disaster Risk Reduction Framework, which had warned for a long period of time of the vulnerability of communities and vital assets because of climate change, had largely been ignored by the Department of Home Affairs.[88]

Even though many countries around the world, including the European Union, the United Kingdom, Canada and New Zealand – as well as 1,480 regional and local governments in 29 countries – have declared a climate emergency, the Australian Government has failed to do so. Climate deniers within that government have positioned those demanding effective action on climate change as 'fanatical' extremists from the left.[89] This is not backed up by evidence as some of the most substantial comments regarding inaction on climate change have come from the former Liberal Prime Minister of Australia Malcolm Turnbull. In an essay written for *Time Magazine* in January 2020, Turnbull claimed that the climate inaction in Australia was because of an alliance of the right-wing politicians, media owned by Rupert Murdoch and vested business interests, especially in the coal industry.[90] In the same month, James Murdoch, son of Rupert Murdoch, accused his family's global media empire of promoting climate denialism.[91]

The climate deniers in the government state that 'the science is not settled' and tell the Australian public that action on climate change will have a negative effect on the economy, leading to the loss of many jobs. As a result, Australia has had no effective energy policy for over 10 years. Senior public servants have been outspoken by what they see as being a story of power and ambition triumphing over the national interest, calling it the greatest public policy failure of their time.[92]

The NCE Summit declaration on failure of leadership stated:

Influential global leaders including political, corporate, media and financial leaders have deliberately refused to accept the overwhelming scientific consensus on climate change and its risks, using predatory delay to prolong an unsustainable economic system. Driven by perverse short-term incentives and lacking the imagination to understand the implications, they have placed humanity in extreme jeopardy.

Many of Australia's leaders are particularly culpable, having done everything possible over the last three decades to prevent the development of serious climate change policy, internationally and domestically, and to protect the fossil fuel industry. Notwithstanding the fact that Australia is the world's fourth largest carbon polluter, exports included, and one of the countries most exposed to climate change.

The first duty of a government is to protect the people, their wellbeing and livelihoods. Instead, Australian governments have left the community largely unprepared for the disasters now unfolding, and for the extensive changes required to maintain a cohesive society as climate change impacts escalate.

… Climate change and its solutions will have profound implications for Australia – its peoples and its lands and waters. It is therefore critical to achieve and secure truly meaningful processes that empower indigenous voices, leadership and knowledge.

... Australians collectively have a duty of care to protect people, nature and civilisation, both locally and globally. Calls to contribute to solutions to the climate threat need to be fair, taking account of people's capacity.[93]

Australia is at a crossroads. If we continue with business as usual, pollution will continue to rise, and the health of the people and the natural world will continue to deteriorate. Many believe there is a window of opportunity, and if the government acts now and implements policies under a strong action scenario, things can be turned around, leading to positives for society, the economy and the environment. There could be an increase in public transport and cleaner energy, making Australia's cities, towns and regions more liveable, smarter and healthier places to be. By embracing these opportunities, Australia could be a world leader and create more than one million jobs by 2040, as well as industries, and be at the forefront of the transition.

Elected leaders have a critical role to play in creating a stable and long-lasting policy framework to grow clean energy and cut pollution. They must set the pathway for Australia to become a net-zero emissions economy and meet our moral obligation to future generations.

Australians have been told that they must choose between jobs or cutting pollution, but research shows this is a false and destructive choice, and that positive economic decisions can be made that support life, not damage it. Political representatives can work with communities and businesses to create a fair and prosperous Australia powered by clean energy. The reality is, there can be a healthy environment and a healthy economy in Australia, or there can be neither.

The NCE Summit identified the following priorities for action:

- Cutting greenhouse gas emissions rapidly to zero. All fossil fuel expansion to be stopped immediately; policies which encourage fossil fuel use halted and subsidies removed; and the existing industry wound down rapidly with adjustment programmes for frontline communities. Strategies to minimise methane emissions need to be implemented urgently.
- Drawing down atmospheric carbon concentrations to a safe level from the current 413 ppm level through actions that include redesigning agricultural and forestry practices and implementing extensive soil, estuarine and ocean carbon sequestration.
- Working to prevent tipping points and damage while the zero emission and drawdown goals are being achieved.
- Integrating adaptation and resilience measures into the economic restructuring needed to restore a safe climate and repair ecosystems.

Early action is essential. The prevalent idea of a gradual transition to net-zero emissions by 2050 is not tenable. A far faster transition is required, using measures appropriate to an existential threat. Climate change must be accepted as an overriding threat to national and human security, with the response being the highest priority at national and global levels.[94]

Role of government

Democracies are based on the premise that governments are made up of representatives voted in by people to make laws in the best interest of society. During the pandemic, it seems that this

has been happening. The government asked the people to change behaviour in order to contain the virus; the people (mostly) complied and the government focused on citizens' wellbeing, with initiatives such as free childcare and wage subsidies, and generous unemployment benefits. It found the old story, which encourages fierce competition and individualism and as little government intervention as possible, did not fit a situation where cooperation and collaboration were the two behaviours needed to overcome a common threat, and the role of government was imperative to survival. This new focus on the role of government has led to people looking more closely at different aspects of government.

Leadership

The pandemic has shown the vital role played by leaders in enabling conditions for a society to cope with a crisis, even to the extent whether they live or die. During the pandemic, Jacinda Ardern, Prime Minister of New Zealand, and Donald Trump, President of the United States, provided a stark contrast in leadership styles. When Prime Minister Ardern was first alerted to the threat posed by the virus, she listened to her health experts, acted decisively, showed empathy and communicated effectively with her people. This led to her country getting behind her so that the impact of the virus was minimised. On the other hand, Donald Trump, taking on a macho strongman version of power, was arrogantly dismissive of advice. When the disaster hit, he chose to blame others rather than take responsibility, and proved impotent to save his people from vast amounts of suffering.

Who does government really serve?

The general lack of engagement in politics by most Australians has meant professionals and the moneyed people have inordinate influence in politics in Australia. Vested interests employ lobbyists to influence the government to make decisions in their favour, rather than what is best for the country.

During the pandemic, the federal government seems to be making decisions for the sake of the common good, and the public has generally applauded their efforts. The popularity of the government has risen. However, there has been a move back to 'business as usual', with a number of representatives from the fossil fuel industry being appointed to the National COVID-19 Commission Advisory Board, whose job it is to steer the country through the recovery period. As banks and shareholders are pulling back from lending money, the fossil fuel industry has been running into difficulties. In the 18 months prior to the pandemic, it suffered one hundred bankruptcies, and gas giants Origin Energy and Santos lost over 10 billion in the last five years on gas and oil projects. However, the presence of its representatives on the commission means it now has the ear of the government, so proposals for huge amounts of taxpayers' money to fund their projects have been put forward.[95]

For a country grappling with the need to act on climate change and the need to move to zero emissions, it is clear these decisions are not in the national interest, and it would be wiser to invest in industries with a future, like renewable energy, which would provide the country with more jobs and cleaner, more affordable energy for all.

Allocation of resources

During the pandemic, many people have become aware of how the decisions a government makes about allocating resources impacts dramatically on their quality of life. Under normal circumstances, governments make decisions about resource allocation based on what they measure, because what they choose to measure is an indication of what they consider important, and it drives political focus and public activity.

The present yardstick for determining the health of Australia's economy and the allocation of resources is the gross national product (GNP). Robert Kennedy stated that the GNP measures everything except those things that make life worth living: the wellbeing of the people and the state of the environment.[96] The budget is a commercial activity and, although crucial to the economy, it is only part of the purpose of government, which is there to serve the wellbeing of the people, rather than create wealth for wealth's sake. Measuring wealth does not measure where the money goes and how it is spent. In Australia, the focus on just building business interests has led to growing inequality as unregulated markets reward greed, power and inherited wealth.

There are leaders who believe that other things should be measured, such as the wellbeing of its citizens and the long-term effect of actions on the sustainability of our planet. At the World Economic Forum in 2019, Jacinda Ardern said her government would introduce a Living Standards Framework based on kindness, wellbeing and empathy, and, in that year, she introduced the Wellbeing Budget, which had as its aim the broadening of the budget's focus beyond economic and fiscal policy. She stated that the Living Standards Framework would be used to inform the government's investment priorities and funding decisions so that they addressed long-term and deep-rooted challenges in society.[97]

This approach makes a lot of sense because, as Katherine Trebeck and Jeremy Williams in their well-researched book, *The Economics of Arrival*, explain, there is a growing realisation that the 'business as usual' approach is leading to diminishing returns on investment as it fails to address social and environmental problems, which are becoming increasingly costly to address.[98]

One underlying assumption of the old story was the belief that people are selfish, and from that cynical view of human nature, the rest followed – privatisation and growing inequality. Now, a new story points to the possibility that humans flourish when they collaborate and cooperate, and an enlightened society is one where sustainable investments are made to secure the future for everyone.

Style of interaction

At the beginning of the pandemic, politicians from all Australian parties worked cooperatively to achieve positive outcomes for the population. It was appreciated by the public because it was different to the aggressive, adversarial style of politicking the country is so used to, and which returned after the initial stages of the pandemic were over. Well-known media personality Lisa Wilkinson wrote the following letter to the Prime Minister Scott Morrison when this style of politicking was blatantly on display during the long and divisive federal election in May 2019:

> Prime Minister, you may have noticed we're all feeling just a little broken right now – broken-hearted in fact, at how toxic the Australian body politic has become – and a return to basic civility in public discourse would be a great start to that healing. We are sick and tired of the energy spent on infighting, political point-scoring and the tribal, factional warfare of recent years. We are aching for inspiring solutions put together by serious people, at a time when we are facing serious problems. Zeroing in on the evermore apparent horrors of climate change, the rising rates of anxiety and depression, homelessness, gender inequality and domestic violence.

She urged the PM to look to building a socially stronger Australia.[99]

Jacinda Ardern has said, 'I really rebel against an idea that politics has to be a place of ego where you are constantly focused on scoring points against each other. Yes, we need a robust democracy, but you can be strong, and you can be kind.'[100] Surely we can emulate that attitude in Australia.

Social inclusion, equality and fairness

One challenge that concerns young people today is inequality. The land of the fair go for all has largely disappeared. In January 2019, Oxfam released startling statistics ahead of the 2020 World Economic Forum, which showed the top one per cent of people in Australia (accounting for around 250,000 people) own roughly USD $1.6 trillion (AUD 2.3 trillion). This is because powerful business interests have worked hard to keep wealth in the hands of a small group. CEO of Oxfam, Lyn Morgain, has stated the 'broken economic system' of the country contributes to the 'poverty and inequality' faced by many Australians.[101]

A long-held belief that economic efficiency and fairness are opposing forces, and achieving one diminishes the other, has sustained this belief. However, there is a growing realisation that social inclusion and connection are not touchy-feely sentiments. People such as leading Australian economist Professor Ian Harper, Dean of Melbourne Business School, says creativity and imagination 'are generally stimulated by human interaction, social creatures that we are'.[102]

SBS network commissioned Deloitte Access Economics to study the economic benefits of improving social inclusion. It found that if business was more socially inclusive, there would be a saving of taxpayers' money, as well as making businesses more productive – which, by Deloitte's modelling, could yield an economic dividend of more than $12 billion a year and would allow individuals to lead happier, more satisfying lives.[103] This would be achieved by affording all people the best opportunities to enjoy life and prosper in society, including Indigenous people, immigrants, women, same-sex couples and people with a physical or mental disability.

They showed that if there was greater social inclusion, people would be less likely to experience discrimination in employment, less likely to experience health issues such as anxiety and depression, and, by lifting wages and workforce participation in districts of socioeconomic disadvantage, the benefits of economic growth would be shared more evenly across the community.[104]

Focusing on fairness would lead to looking at the remuneration people receive for the work they do. During the crisis, the mismatch has become clearer between the incomes of essential workers, such as childcare workers, teachers, nurses, check-out staff, police and community workers – all of whom put their lives at risk for the sake of the community – and the exorbitant salaries of entertainers and sportspeople, who are not needed at the time.

Racism

During the pandemic crisis in June 2020, the killing of African American man George Floyd at the hands of police in Minneapolis triggered massive social unrest in the US. However, this event led to a heightened awareness of problems faced by First Nations people in Australia too because of systemic biases, particularly in the justice system.

The first settlement of Australia was founded on colonialism. Lt James Cook was an English explorer. His 1768–71 voyage of exploration sailed under the instructions to take possession of the Southern Continent if it was uninhabited, or with the consent of the natives if it was occupied. Either way, it was to be taken. Upon his arrival, Lt Cook declared the land he called New South Wales to be the property of Britain's King George III, and ignored the inconvenient fact that the land was already well-populated. His failure to even attempt to gain the consent of the Indigenous peoples began the fiction that Australia was waste and unoccupied, or 'terra nullius'.[105]

It was the beginning of the deterioration of the quality of life for the First Nations people of this land, and this has been demonstrated by their levels of incarceration. First Nations people in Australia are the most incarcerated people *globally*, surpassing the rates of African American people in the United States. In 2019, for every 100,000 First Nations adults, 2,481 are in prisons, compared with 164 non-Indigenous people. This means that despite comprising two per cent of the general adult population, First Nations Australians comprise 28 per cent of the prison population. For First Nations women, the rate is 33 per cent, and they are 21 times more likely to be imprisoned than non-Indigenous women.[106] A high number of deaths occur when Indigenous people are in custody. In 1991, the fact that there had been 99 deaths in custody led to the establishment of the Royal Commission into Aboriginal Deaths in Custody. However, since that time, 432 Indigenous people have died in custody. No-one has been prosecuted.

Racism is a running sore in Australia. Reconciliation must occur and live in the hearts, minds and actions of all Australians. The country must move forward to create a nation that is strengthened by respect, fairness and justice for Aboriginal and Torres Strait Islander people.

Observations from yours truly, a Youth

Ciara M. Symons

Now, I stumble my way towards **global anxieties***. And what a mess we've made. This is the blaring bad news bordered in red on your TV screens:*

'BREAKING NEWS – EXTINCTION IS RIGHT AROUND THE CORNER FOR ONE MILLION SPECIES'

Yet for some people, it is simply 'fixed' by blocking it out of our minds. We have stopped listening. You see, this is what we've done: we have made the act of ignoring more accessible. Science and ethics are now toys you get to pick up and put down whenever you want. For some reason, opinion rivals evidence. Opinion rivals human rights.

I think Socrates would have wept at today's society. So many people know his name, but not what he aimed to achieve. You shouldn't know his name; you should know his philosophy:

To challenge social norms.

Socrates took hold of a concept by its roots. He questioned why it was there and who had planted it. If the concept wasn't nourishing anyone, or he felt it was unjust, he'd try to yank it out. But the roots were always too strong and required a team. Yet not enough people cared to help.

What can we learn from this? That we can yank these colossal concepts out if the team is large enough. If the team works together.

But you've seen what happens when a group of people try to change the social norms. It often starts with ignorance, it leads to protests, and eventually turns into a battlefield. There is no rationality on a battlefield. There is no philosophy on a battlefield – only blood and bloodlust.

We have so many young Socrates in the world now. But too many bystanders want them to shut up. And not unlike the original Socrates, they are being led to an early deathbed – unless the team grows.

Comparison is deceptively deadly. It is so easy to say, 'It could be worse. I've got it good compared to others.' There is so much to be grateful for. It can make one guilty for wanting more. I have a roof, I have food, I have safety. But I am more than that. I am more aware than that. I should not feel guilty for wanting others to be safe. You should not tell me to stand down because of what I already have.

I have a lot of demands for society. I could list them for you.

But this is the one I will go with: I want my vote to be for a government that seeks justice for the people. Justice for Earth, our home. I want a philosophy-led government.

Don't believe that is possible? Think of Marcus Aurelius. Aurelius ruled for the people, not for his own wanton need for power. Why did we lose this, this justice for the people? Why do we now scoff at philosophy when it is the study of thinking? It is ironic for the mindless to look down upon such an art. And maybe that's just why – it's an art.

We do not hold The Arts in such a glorious light as we used to – Science took over much of our interest. I don't blame it – we have vaccines, medical wonders, we have been to the moon, and we plan to go to the red speck in the sky we call Mars. We have progress – but what do we progress for if we leave behind our purpose in life?

What is our purpose? I am not even two decades old, and yet I propose that I have the answer. It's because the answer is simple:

We must create.

I could try and word this in my own way, but it is so eloquently stated by the character John Keating in Dead Poets Society*:*

'Medicine, law, business, engineering, these are noble pursuits and necessary to sustain life. But poetry, beauty, romance, love, these are what we stay alive for.'

These words are my mantra. And it's not just poetry; this luxurious phrase is the essence of all The Arts. To feel is to be alive, to be entirely human. To try and suffocate any emotion out of yourself is to crack into fragments. But that is exactly what happens if we do not take The Arts seriously – we will crack and crumble, leaving behind our humanity like a snake's dead skin.

Roaring Twenties

By Ciara M. Symons

When was our last revolution?
High time,
high time
we alight a new day;
Let's overthrow, let's overrule!

I wanted a new day,
as we entered a new decade;
I wanted a fresh start,
but I was not expecting this:

The same smoky dusk
with the same smoky dawn;
Gaia's plague being flushed with fire,
    with disease?
Destruction fought
        with destruction;

Hasn't Pan caused such a Panic?

Like a held breath,
We'll either scream
        or sigh;
Revolt
or resign?
Ride down with our wraths?
Lie down,
let's rest boys,
let's rest;
Leave it be.

Let's raise an era of Titans –
An era of Atlases!
Yes, yes,
        leave it to *them*,
Let's leave our descendants
to hold the
    weight of the world!

Let's not take
        Any part in it,
No, no;
Let's leave –
Out of sight,
        out of mind.
Such role models,
                Such role models...

We are the
Generation of Atlas.

Atlas did not choose to
        hold the skies;
                He was stuck there;
                Stuck.   Stuck.   Stuck.

He is Endurance,
                but even Endurance fades;
He will exhaust,
                We will exhaust.

we do not fight this fight
        – hold this sky –
out of want,
        out of desire;
we hold it because
no one else
        will.

This was Atlas' *punishment* –
Is it humanity's too?

Is this how we fall into chaos?
                Madness?
Mad. *Mad.*
This is Madness.
MAD.
We are   *mad.*
a
Murkyyy mudddyyy mAD (abandon ship,)
Is this howw   (abandon ship,)
    AtlaS   (no longer do   )
felT   (these bright   )
    WhEn he was   (sails fly...   )
            AbanDonnED?

60

When was our last revolution?
High time,
high time
we alight a new day;
Let's overthrow, let's overrule!

I was not expecting this,
not today
not *today*.

why
does humanity
decide
to decompose
NOW?
    (or has it always been rotten to the
                       cORE?)

So,
    this is our Roaring Twenties?
        plightandpain;
        plightandpain;

Let's get booz-ay
           booz-ay
   booz-ay

Panic! no more

Hell,
let's dance our days away!

Endurance? Who cares;
Atlas? Who's *that?*

If this is the end of the line,
Let's go out
      Roaring our
         plightsandpains
           Away...

(Abandon ship,)
(Abandon ship,)
(No longer do)
(These bright)
(Sails fly.)

'[...] the reversed Fool can show that
you are taking too many risks and acting
recklessly. In your attempt to live 'in
the moment' and be spontaneous and
adventurous, you may do so in total
disregard of the consequences of your
actions and engaging in activities that put
both yourself and others at risk.'

'At its worst, the reversed Magician
signifies greed, manipulation and trickery.
You may be masterful at manifesting, but
if you are out of touch with your Higher
Self, you may only do it for your personal
gain and at the expense of others.'

61

Compromise

I've got a
problem with
people
Calling a
virus
A "war".

What is War?
When two sides
      are sentient,
When two sides
      are too ignorant
      to see
That they should just
let whatever it is
      be.

COMPROMISE
Is the word War never learnt.

COMPROMISE
Is what we plead for
But never receive.

What is Pestilence?
It dwindles, decays and
destroys things quickly.
Yes, it is an acid.
Not a force
you can
      bargain with;
      Compromise with —
and there are no
      deluded men
Sitting at
 the head of a
(square,
      not round)
 table
Thinking that
all the lives lost
Was worth his
w i n n i n g s .

Not many people
      want war;
But even less
want disease.

Who is Nature?
 The one you
 don't dispute.
 She gives the
 warning calls,
C O M P R O M I S E .
COMPROMISE.
COMPROMISE.

Perhaps
she got sick of calling out.
Perhaps
At the end of this,
We'll finally learn.

So,
Is the virus a war?

            No.
There is normality
      in Humanity
      murdering itself.
      And that is war.

So, I guess
Death is just
A forgettable
character,
isn't he?

"Treat others the
way you'd like
to be treated"
Oh, how Nature
knows this well.

As soon as She
   Assigns Death
   A new face
- The fear spikes
(this time with
      the death tally).
So now
q u a n t i t y
is a worry to you?

         "ONE HUNDRED
         TWENTY-SIX
         THOUSAND
         FIVE HUNDRED
         AND THIRTY-NINE
               AND
         COUNTING
LADIES AND GENTLEMEN"

(We forget
How much worse
We can be
to ourselves.)

So, I guess
Humanity
Will keep
Skipping
To this
dance macabre,
and
at midnight,
at the deepest
trough of
energy and
enthusiasm,
Death will
Scoop
Humanity
up,
and bring them
to Nature's bed,
with all the bugs
that bite.

So, who
Will you
bargain
with?

The one that
hears
But doesn't truly
listen?
Or
The one that
warned us
but,
wasn't heard?

Three Greek Ladies, ready to be revived

Is THIS the
REVOLUTION
I cried
"high time
High TIME"
For?
Why,
This ugly picture –
Did you not expect it?
Has history taught you NOTHING?

The change won't be sudden,
Because we live in reality, dear boy.
The change won't be today,
Nor tomorrow...
They say Rome wasn't
Built in a day.
(And it takes longer to reform an entirely
backwards country
In this modern madness).

Do you choose to *ignore*
The change that will rise
 with our heat,
With our wrath and
 with our rage
        – Like the stormy phoenix
Spitting lava from her tongue?

Today, I don't speak as myself,
I do not speak *for* myself;
I am merely the messenger for those
Who seek to execute the tyranny.
What do we want?
JUSTICE.
When do we want it?

When do *we get* it?

We didn't get it then,
With ladies wearing trousers
With the men holding their boys,
With the women holding their gals,
NOT EVEN when the slaves could
Turn into their own selves.
THESE WERE *FRAGMENTS*.
There is no humanity in just
fragments;
IT IS ALL OR NOTHING.
Now, we demand in *full*.

GIVE US THEMIS.
HAND US NIKE.
BRING ON NEMESIS.

63

Poem notes:

Roaring Twenties

This poem was a response to the beginning of 2020. The bushfires could be smelt as the smoke clung to the air. COVID-19 was also starting to be taken more seriously. When I wrote this poem, it was around the time when the events were overlapping and wholly overwhelming. Entering the new decade, it felt like it was supposed to be a point where we could finally reflect and take action against our massive crises, like climate change. But that ideal collapsed quickly. The poem took shape as an expression of my feelings: anger, distress and futility. I entwined the novel themes of the 1920s to add a kind of frenzied, reckless feeling.

> *The Greek mythological figures in this poem are:*
> * *Gaia – the primordial deity/personification of the Earth.*
> * *Pan – the god of nature and the wild.*
> * *Atlas – the Titan god of endurance, largely recognised as the god that holds up the skies.*

Compromise

This poem is a discussion as I try to articulate my thoughts on how poorly we – humanity – dealt with the threat of COVID-19. The poem also makes more general observations on how we perceive war and plague. This discussion takes the form of a warning, personifying Nature, Humanity and Death.

Three Greek Ladies, ready to be revived

This poem was the result of my thoughts being stirred by the Black Lives Matter protests. It is my demand for overall change and reform. The beginning of the poem calls back to my previous poem Roaring Twenties.

> *The Greek mythological figures in this poem are:*
> * *Themis – a Titaness; the goddess of divine order, fairness, law, natural law.*
> * *Nike – the goddess of victory.*
> * *Nemesis – the goddess who enacts retribution against those who succumb to hubris (arrogance before the gods).*

Part II

Chapter 5:
The heart

Your vision will become clear only when you can look into your own heart. He who looks outside, dreams; he who looks inside, awakes.
Carl Jung

The new story is ready to be told, but the challenge that faces us is learning how to amplify it so that it is strong enough to inspire and guide society. The truth is, if facts and statistics could fix things, things would already be fixed. Albert Einstein once observed, 'No problem can be solved at the same level of consciousness which created it.'

Is it possible, then, that the new consciousness we are seeking could come from a different place, from a greater understanding of the heart?

To humans, the heart has always been a source of fascination. As a physical organ, it beats 100,000 times a day, sending 2,000 gallons of blood through the intricate blood vessels that, if stretched end to end, would cover 60,000 miles, more than twice the circumference of the Earth.[107] However, the world's languages are filled with idioms of the heart, which give it more significance than just a physical organ. When people are sincere, they are said to be 'speaking from the heart'. When they are passionate, they are said to be 'doing something with their whole heart'. When a person betrays their own interest, we say they were thinking 'with their head not their heart'. When a person is in despair, they are said to be 'downhearted'.

In January 2019, excited journalists and commentators were ecstatic at the tremendous courage and tenacity displayed by young tennis player Alex de Minaur in a gruelling five-set match against the ferocious Henri Laaksonen at the Australian Open. The day after, they hit the papers with headlines like 'The kid's all heart' and 'Alex Minaur wins a nation's heart with the Australian Open run'.

For centuries, poets and philosophers have sensed that the heart is a source of wisdom. When the Indigenous people of Australia wanted to tell the nation of their deepest desire for the future, they put forward the Uluru Statement from the Heart. Aristotle considered the heart to be 'the centre of reason, thought and emotion, senior to the brain in its importance'. Ninth century Arabic philosopher Abu Nasr al-Farabi believed that 'The ruling organ in the human body is the heart; the brain is a secondary ruling organ subordinated to the heart.' Auguste Comte, a 19th century French philosopher, declared that the brain should be servant to the heart. Blaise Pascal (1623–1662), a French mathematician, physicist and religious philosopher, stated, 'We know the truth not only by reason but also by the heart.'[108]

In many cultures, both ancient and modern, the heart is seen as the seat of the soul, the secret place where the spirit dwells and is the engine room of emotions, which lead to the positive actions of love, kindness, wisdom, compassion and courage.

Hebrew, Christian, Hindu and Islamic traditions focus on the heart as the primary organ for influencing and directing morality and decision-making. In the Christian tradition, Proverbs 23:7 says, 'For as a man thinketh in his heart so is he.' In the New Testament, Luke 5:22 says, 'What reason ye in your hearts?' In the Jewish tradition Kabbalah, the heart is seen as the central sphere, which holds the key to the mysteries of health, joy and wellbeing. In Yogic practice, the physical heart is seen as the guide to the internal guru.[109]

In the West, even though there are many references to the heart throughout the language, they are seen as figurative. In the field of medicine, the heart is seen merely as a multi-chambered muscular pump criss-crossed by electrical circuitry. However, in other cultures, there is belief that there is a connection between the heart and the head. In traditional Chinese medicine, for example, the heart is seen as the seat of the mind, and the body forms a bridge between the two. It is believed that the heart houses the *shen*, which can be translated as both mind and spirit. Thus the mind or spirit is housed in the heart, and the blood vessels are the communication channels that carry the heart's vital rhythm messages throughout the body, keeping everything working in synchronicity.[110] An ancient Chinese dictionary describes the silk thread that connects the brain and the heart, and in the Japanese language, there are two distinct words to describe the heart: *shinzu* denotes the physical organ, and *kokora* refers to the mind of the heart.[111]

In the last few decades, the West and scientists have started to ask more questions about the heart's functioning. In the 1970s, research by physiologists John and Beatrice Lacey, at the Fels Research Institute, found that when the brain sent orders to the heart, the heart does not automatically obey but could act independently, and though the heartbeat usually sped up when the brain sent an arousal signal to the body in response

67

to stimuli, there were times when it slowed down while other organs responded with arousal. They also found that the heart seemed to send messages to the brain that could influence behaviour.[112]

In other research, neuroscientists have found that the heart has an independent, complex nervous system, referred to as the 'brain in the heart', and that this system has at least 40,000 neurons (nerve cells), which is as many as is found in the various subcortical centres in the brain. It appears there is a two-way communication system between the heart and the brain, and neural connections go from the heart to the brain rather than the other way around.[113] Both thoughts and feelings can be powerful, but a strong emotion can silence thought. You can rarely think yourself out of a strong emotion, and the strongest emotions trigger ruminating or incessant thought.

Emotional intelligence and the wisdom of the heart

From the beginning of the 20th century, researchers have sought to understand the nature of intelligence. In Western culture, a person's intelligence has been equated with their spatial, numerical and linguistic abilities used to solve a wide range of logical problems and develop strategic thinking, which results in a measure known as the Intelligence Quotient, or IQ. It has been nurtured by Western school systems and has dominated Western business.

In 1985, psychologist Howard Gardner discovered that as well as logical, mathematical and spatial intelligence, there are other intelligences, such as musical, body, kinaesthetic, intrapersonal and interpersonal. In 1996, Daniel Goleman identified an emotional intelligence (EQ), which is the capacity of individuals to recognise their own emotions and those of others, discern between different feelings, label them appropriately and use that emotional information to guide thinking and behaviour. This leads to self-awareness and sensitivity to others.

The American scientific organisation the HeartMath Institute has extensively researched many different aspects of the heart, and has put forward the proposition that access to the wisdom of the heart strengthens a person's EQ. They have found that when a person learns to decipher the messages from the heart, they can use this information to deal with life's situations and challenges in a balanced and coherent way. Without this guiding influence, people can easily fall prey to reactive emotions, such as insecurity, anger, fear, hate and blame, resulting in negative reactions and toxic interactions with others.[114]

Religious traditions have long taught the importance of the heart, and many compassionate people and movements have emerged from those traditions. However, now that we understand what a vital part the heart plays in the personal and collective wellbeing of our society, I believe it is time to take the heart out of the realm of religion and philosophy and embed its wisdom into the way we order our society. We can do this by reclaiming the *language of the heart*, made up of the following elements:

- Hope
- Empathy
- Action
- Relationships
- Trust

We need to make this the predominant language used to shape our society. For this to happen, we may need to change the mindset of our country.

Australian social researcher Hugh Mackay, after extensive research across Australia, identified three main mindsets in Australia:

1. The **self-absorbed mindset**, where people filter every situation through the lens of 'what is in it for me – my happiness, my entitlements, my comfort?'
2. The **moral mindset**, which is based on a rigid set of rules and ideas about what constitutes goodness. Those with this mindset aim to impose those rules and ideas onto others.
3. The **compassionate mindset**. People who have this mindset take the pursuit of goodness for granted, and kindness is their currency for dealing with other people, especially those who are different. Generosity of spirit, openness and personal warmth underpins all their interactions with others, and there is an acceptance of the value of every person. People with this mindset are compelled to serve the deeper concerns of humanity and the planet, and they share the values of justice, kindness, inclusivity and respect. They focus on collaboration, connection, friendship and equality even though they may have different political and religious views. People with this mindset speak the language of the heart.[115]

A great example of a person who exemplifies the compassionate mindset was Ted Noffs, who established the Wayside Chapel in Sydney in the 1960s. Ted started his career as a Methodist Minister, but he shifted to a more expansive way of thinking later in life where he came to believe that all humans, at a spiritual level, are part of the Family of Humanity. This was captured in his statement: '… no-one is a stranger to me … I am a Protestant and Catholic, a Jew and a Muslim'.[116]

'Love over Hate' is the motto for the Wayside Chapel, which still exists. It provides services to vulnerable members of the community. It proudly states that it is a safe community where there is no 'us and them' because the barriers of judgement have been broken down, people from all walks of life are welcome, and love prevails. It aims to be the intersection between love and hate, faith and no faith, the haves and the have-nots, the housed and the homeless, the sick and the well. Everyone is treated with respect, and a person struggling is seen as a person to be met, not a problem to be solved.[117]

Chapter 6: The heart's language

Hope is not a fool's pact; it is a pact with our best selves, the one we allow to be seen in quiet and hidden moments. **Kon Karapanagiotidis**

Hope

Social justice advocate Tim Costello, during a discussion regarding the unemployment benefit New Start on the national television program *Q&A*, stated that the low rate of that benefit, at that time, was a factor in Australia's youth suicide epidemic because young people, being forced to live on $40 a day, had developed a profound sense of hopelessness. He stated:

> The fundamental question all humans ask is, *do I matter*? Hopelessness comes when you think you don't count, and people being condemned to live below the poverty line know they're expendable, they're dispensable, and don't matter.[118]

Adolescence is a time of fun and growing maturity, but it can also be a time of anxiety, confusion and overwhelm. Young people have energy and ideas, but if hope is lost, they are crushed. They wait and watch to see how the world treats them.

In 1990, a group of Canadian researchers explored the Circle of Courage. This Native American concept maintains that there is a Circle of Needs that must be met for a young person to feel 'encouraged' and optimistic about life. If those needs are not met, the circle is broken, and the young person feels 'discouraged'. They believed that for a young person to have a sense of hope, they must:

- feel valued, connected, affirmed and safe so that they establish a sense of being significant and valued
- have a sense of mastery and competence, which is recognised by others
- have a sense of independence, which gives them a sense of agency and the power to make their own decisions and influence the decisions of others.

Researchers found that if these needs are not met, and young people lose hope, they will try to meet them in a distorted way. Trying to gain a sense of belonging, they join a gang; trying to establish power, they become bullies; and trying to gain mastery, they become involved in risky or anti-social activities.[119] There is a lot of truth in the African proverb: *The child who is not embraced by the village will burn it down to feel its warmth.*

Young people want a predictable world, but no-one can promise them that, as life is complex and often does not turn out as we expect. However, adults can help them develop hope by encouraging them to move from a fixed mindset, where they believe things can never change when things go wrong, to a growth mindset, where they believe they have agency and can influence their destiny by facing and overcoming challenges when they arise. Adults can help them identify their strengths and help them build on these to establish resilience, and they can share stories of people who have overcome difficulties. With hope in their hearts, young people can face the toughest of situations.

Empathy

Love and compassion are necessities, not luxuries. Without them, mankind cannot survive. **Dalai Lama**

When renowned neuroscientist Richard Davidson first began studying compassion, it was with Tibetan monks, who were long-time meditators. The monks were asked to wear a cap with electroencephalogram (EEG) electrodes in it to measure their compassion. When they heard this, they all began laughing. The researchers thought it was because the cap looked funny as all the electrodes were connected to a trailing wire, resembling a wild wig. However, the laughter of the monks wasn't because of the cap. The researchers had it all wrong. A monk finally explained, 'Everyone knows compassion doesn't arise from the brain; it comes from the heart.'[120]

Empathy is the main building block of compassion. It is the emotional skill that allows a person to walk in the shoes of another person and respond to them in a meaningful and caring way. When someone shows empathy, it helps the person over a threshold that they might otherwise never have crossed on their own. Everyone has times of great uncertainty in their life, and if they are left alone at such a time, they can have a great sense of confusion. When empathy is shown, they can have a sense of light instead, and begin to find the stairs and the door out of the dark. There is no judgement but words of relief and release.

Empathy is an expression of shared humanity and is different from pity, which can diminish the dignity of the recipient. In her book *Any Ordinary Day*, Leigh Sales explored the effect of traumatic events on a wide range of people and her own ordeal during the birth of her second child. She observed that the friends she appreciated most were not the charismatic

ones who made her laugh, but, rather, those who showed true empathy. She came to believe that among all the good human qualities there is none greater than kindness.[121]

One of the greatest expressions of empathy by a leader was shown by PM Jacinda Ardern in March 2019 when a white supremacist massacred 50 innocent Muslims attending a prayer session at two mosques in the city of Christchurch, New Zealand. After the terrible event, she told them that even though others could not know their grief, the country would walk with them at every stage. She told them they would be surrounded by *aroha, manaakitanga,* Maori words for kindness, compassion and generosity.[122]

Empathy and wellbeing

In 2016, Dr Katherine Nelson, Assistant Professor of Psychology at Sewanee: The University of the South, Tennessee, undertook a study that showed how practising acts of kindness or showing empathy improved mood and overall wellbeing. In her experiment, 473 volunteers were separated into four groups. Each group had to complete different tasks over six weeks. One group was asked to complete acts that improved the community, such as picking up rubbish. The second group performed acts of kindness where they showed empathy for other people, such as buying a friend a cup of coffee or helping a family member cook dinner. The third group was instructed to perform acts of kindness for themselves, such as exercising more or taking a day off from work. Finally, the fourth group was the control group who did nothing out of their ordinary activities.

Before and after the six weeks, all participants filled out a questionnaire to assess their psychological, emotional and social wellbeing. They also self-reported their positive and negative emotions weekly throughout the study. It was found that those who were involved in prosocial behaviour experienced greater positive emotion, improved moods and wellbeing, whereas those assigned to engage in self-focused behaviour did not report any improved wellbeing or positive emotions.[123]

Dr Dacher Keltner, Professor of Psychology at the University of California, Berkeley, has found that performing acts of kindness and empathy can activate the release of dopamine, a feel-good neurotransmitter, in the brain, and it can lead to us feeling as if we are serving something larger than the self.[124]

There is a growing body of research that shows how compassion and empathy could be the keys to improved health, wellbeing and longevity. Brain imaging reveals that exercising compassion stimulates the same pleasure centres associated with the drive for food, water and sex.[125] Dr James Doty, Professor of Neurosurgery at Stanford University, believes people are much happier and live better lives if they are compassionate.[126]

Teaching children empathy

If empathy is so important, how do we teach it to our children? Richard Davidson has stated that research shows all children have the potential to show kindness and empathy but that not all children are kind or empathetic. He likens children learning empathy to children learning language because even though all children have a propensity for language, a child needs to be in a normal linguistic community for that propensity to be expressed – they absorb it from the people around them like plants osmotically absorb sunlight. There are case studies of feral children who, having been raised in the wild, do not develop normal language. Davidson says it is the same with kindness and empathy. Children need to be in an empathetic and kind environment for the potential of empathy to be realised because their behaviour and attitudes mirror what they see around them.[127]

In Denmark, schools have made empathy a fundamental part of the curriculum because it is considered as important as subjects such as English and Mathematics. One hour a week is dedicated to the 'Klassens tid', an empathy lesson for students aged six to 16 years. During the session, whole classes interact with each other on a personal level, discussing their problems with each other and the teacher, whether they are related to school or not, in order to find a solution. If there are no problems to discuss, children simply spend the time together relaxing and enjoying *hygge*. This is a word that cannot be translated literally since it is a phenomenon closely related to Danish culture, but it could be defined as intentionally 'created intimacy', where friendship is shared in a welcoming and intimate atmosphere. It is a fundamental concept for the Danish sense of wellbeing.[128]

In order to understand how Danes teach empathy, Danish psychotherapist Iben Sandahl has conducted field research in schools. She found that most of the tasks in school are carried out by teams, and students are taught that the focus is not to excel over others but rather to try to improve themselves. Their progress in a subject is measured exclusively in relation to themselves. As a result, Danish schools do not give prizes or trophies to students who excel in school subjects or sports. Sandahl also found that schools use a collaborative approach to learning, which consists of bringing together children with different strengths and weaknesses in different subjects to work on projects. Children are encouraged to see that they get better results if they help each other. This approach develops empathy.[129]

In 2008, Melbourne teacher Hugh Van Cuylenburg volunteered to teach in a small, poor Indian school in the Ladakh region in India. The school lacked the kind of resources any school in Australia would take for granted, but, to his surprise, he found the students were the happiest children he had ever met. This was a stark contrast to many students in the elite school where he taught, who suffered depression and anxiety. He believed the happiness of the Indian children came from the fact that their families, even though they faced hardships every day, had taught them the importance of gratitude, mindfulness and empathy.[130]

Action

Unless someone like you cares an awful lot, nothing is going to get better. It's not. **The Lorax by Dr. Seuss**

Central to the heart's language is people taking action to make the world a better place. Below are some significant actions taken by people overseas.

The issue: gun violence in the US

Gun violence is an entrenched problem in the United States, and school shootings are common. At least 15,292 people were fatally shot in the US in 2019, excluding suicides, according to data gathered by Gun Violence Archive, a non-profit that tracked shootings at a three per cent increase over 2018.

The action

Following the school shooting on 14 February, 2018, at the Marjory Stoneman Douglas High School in Parkland, Florida, where 17 students and teachers were killed in a gun rampage, American students mobilised around gun laws in the #MarchForOurLives movement. The movement started with The National Walkout when nearly one million students walked out from their classes for exactly 17 minutes (one for each of the victims of the massacre) on the one-month anniversary of the shooting.

On 24 March, 2018, a main event was staged in Washington, but there were 880 sibling events throughout the US and around the world. At the march in Washington, students began by observing 17 minutes of silence with their backs to the White House. One of the most powerful moments of the march was when Parkland shooting survivor Emma Gonzalez made the following statement:

> Six minutes and about twenty seconds. In a little over six minutes, 17 of our friends were taken from us, 15 were injured, and everyone, absolutely everyone, was forever altered. Everyone who was there understands, everyone who has been touched by the cold grip of gun violence understands … No-one could comprehend the devastating aftermath or how far this would reach or where this would go. For those who still can't comprehend because they refuse to, I'll tell you where it went. Right into the ground, six feet deep.[131]

After listing the names of her classmates and teachers who died that day, she stopped speaking and stared into the crowd for four minutes with tears streaming down her face. She ended the silence with the words:

> Since the time that I came out here, it has been six minutes and twenty seconds. The shooter has ceased shooting and will soon abandon his rifle, blend in with the students as they escape, and walk free for an hour before arrest. Fight for your lives before it's someone else's job.[132]

At the march were siblings of students who had been killed in other school massacres, including the brother of a victim of the Sandy Hook Elementary School shooting, which occurred in December 2012, in Newtown, Connecticut, when a gunman killed 26 people, including 20 children between six and seven years old.

The protesters urged for universal background checks on all gun sales, raising the federal age of gun ownership and possession to 21, closing of the gun show loophole, a restoration of the 1994 Federal Assault Weapons Ban, and a ban on the sale of high-capacity magazines and bump stocks in the US. Turnout was estimated to be between 1.2 and 2 million people in the US, making it one of the largest protests in American history.

The issue: climate change

As mentioned earlier in this book, one of the most significant challenges facing the world today is climate change.

The action: Project Drawdown

In 2014, environmentalist Paul Hawken viewed the climate challenge and asked himself the following question: Is it game over or game on? He decided the latter, as he believed that stopping global warming is possible because scientific evidence has shown solutions already exist that could make it possible. He wanted to shift the global conversation about climate change away from 'doom and gloom' defeatism to one of possibility, opportunity, action and empowerment. He founded an organisation, named Project Drawdown – drawdown being the term used to describe a point in time when the concentration of greenhouse gases in the Earth's atmosphere begin to decline on a year-to-year basis.

The organisation works with a coalition of scholars, scientists, entrepreneurs and advocates from across the globe to help develop realistic, solution-specific models, technical assessments and policy memos projecting the financial and climactic impacts of existing solutions. Project Drawdown's role is not to implement these solutions, but rather to point to how they are already being implemented by humanity around the

globe, and the potential of these solutions if they are scaled over the next 30 years.

The organisation has reviewed, analysed and identified the most viable global climate solutions in the vital areas of food, energy, land use, gender equity, materials and liveable cities, and has shared these findings with the world. These cover: clean, renewable energy, including solar and wind; green buildings, both new and retrofitted; efficient transportation from Brazil to China; thriving ecosystems through protection and restoration; reducing waste and reclaiming its value; growing food in good ways that regenerate soil; and shifting diets to less meat, more plants. The organisation has identified 100 solutions, 80 of which are already in operation and 20 are gaining traction.[133]

The issue: sharing information for the common good

There is an assumption in our society that all information of value must be protected through excessive patents, copyright and intellectual property rights so that profit can be made from that information. This means that material that could be of value to serve the common good is not freely available and usable.

The action: the Peer to Peer movement

The Peer to Peer (P2P) Foundation, founded by Michel Bauwens, James Burke and Brice Le Blévennec, puts forward a new way of achieving outcomes in the business world.

The movement challenges the idea that there is only one way to do business and that every transaction must be for profit. It has set up alternative communication systems promoting the free exchange of knowledge and services of value with free/open source software and hardware. Examples of things shared include culture and open access to education and science resources. These are shared between peers, and the focus is on distributing and sharing knowledge of value for the common good. The movement believes that humans flourish when they work together, so it encourages collaboration and cooperation. Products are judged on their value to a community rather than their market value and potential to make a profit. All actions are thought through for their social and environmental impact. The movement believes in widespread participation and encourages individual movements that are participatory and grassroots rather than top-down.[134]

Relationships

I've learned that people will forget what you said, people will forget what you did, but people will never forget how you made them feel.
Maya Angelou

In 1938, an ambitious study known as the Harvard Study of Adult Development commenced, and for 75 years the study tracked the lives of 724 Harvard graduates and other men who lived in the inner-city, asking about their work, their home lives and their health. The researchers wanted to know what contributed to their satisfaction with life. They found that participants who had good social connections with family, friends and the general community were physically healthier and lived longer than those who were less connected.

These close relationships, more than money or fame, kept the participants happy throughout their lives, protecting them from life's discontents, helping delay mental and physical decline, and served as a better predictor of long and happy lives than social class, IQ, cholesterol levels or even genes. It seems that humans

are wired for social connection and are at their best when being cooperative and caring about each other. Other research also shows that isolation and loneliness put people at far greater risk of early disease than smoking. Authentic social connections have a profound effect on mental health, which exceeds the value of exercise and ideal body weight on physical health. One of the major findings from the Harvard study was that the quality of relationships was important if the participants were to experience the benefits they offered.[135]

Developing authentic relationships with young people

Research has shown that one of the most important contributors to the wellbeing of vulnerable young people is a one-on-one relationship with a caring adult outside the family. A mentor is a person willing to take on that role. Some young people have natural mentors, but many do not. Mentoring programs are set up to recruit caring community members to set up safe relationships for young people.

For many years, I was a teacher at Baimbridge College in Hamilton, south-western Victoria. I knew many students in my classes could benefit from these kinds of relationships, so, working closely with the community and other members of staff, I set up the Standing Tall mentoring program at the school. The experience taught me a lot about what it takes to develop a positive relationship with a young person. The relationships bought new meaning to the words 'you raise me up to more than I can be'. One of the most successful was the relationship between Dylan and his mentor Heather*.

Dylan was a capable student in my Year 10 class who had big dreams, but things happening in his home life worked against him achieving those dreams. Dylan and his brother lived with their mother, who struggled to stay on top of things, and the family was evicted from rental properties on a number of occasions. There were rumours about his mother circulating in the community. When she was charged with stealing pension cheques from a vulnerable neighbour, nobody was surprised.

A heavy sense of sadness surrounded Dylan, and in class he always sat alone. In the middle of the year, I convinced him to enter the mentoring program and was thrilled when he was matched with Heather, a warm-hearted local café owner. With Heather by his side, things turned around, and on leaving school, Dylan achieved his impossible dream of going on to university.

Watching their relationship taught me what it takes to develop a successful relationship with a young person.

* For the sake of privacy, real names have not been used.

Reciprocity

For a relationship to have energy and meaning, there needs to be a strong sense of reciprocity. When Heather and Dylan's relationship started, Heather saw Dylan's strength and determination and was determined to give him the support and encouragement he so desperately needed. However, as she came to know him, she came to enjoy his company, his gentle sense of humour and his insightful observations about life. They both loved cooking, and preparing culinary delights became a highlight of their mentoring sessions. Heather struggled with using her computer, so she was pleased when Dylan taught her how to use it so she could use the internet and stay in touch with her grandchildren. What developed between Heather and Dylan was a true friendship.

Non-judgement

Appearance, social class, age and reputation can be barriers when people meet, but Heather, though well aware of Dylan's home situation, approached the relationship with an open mind and heart. Unlike many in the community, she passed no judgement and made him feel worthy and valued.

True listening

The Dalai Lama once said, 'When you talk you are only repeating what you already know, but if you listen you may learn something new.' Like every young person, Dylan yearned to be listened to and taken seriously. Through listening to Dylan, Heather came to understand the things that troubled him, the challenges he faced, the things that interested him, and what he wanted to achieve in his life, and she came to appreciate him as the highly intelligent and complex character he was.

Respect

Respect from the community was not something Dylan had learned to expect. Heather was able to turn that around the night she took him to the local Rotary Club and introduced him to the members. They invited him to speak about his dreams. The respect that he was afforded by the group proved to be a turning point for Dylan, and we could see his confidence grow after that experience. When Dylan left school, he wrote the following letter to show his appreciation:

> I would like to say that I am a student who has benefited from mentoring. I am studying biotechnology at university. My mentor, Heather, has been important in helping achieve this. There are probably quite a few students who, in their last years of secondary education,

do not believe in themselves enough to continue, let alone consider themselves eligible for future tertiary education. This is likely to be due to family problems, living situations, or suffering misleading intimidation. Heather helped me conquer my adversities by providing valuable encouragement and allowing me to explore my future possibilities.

Trust

You must trust and believe in people or life becomes impossible.
Anton Chekhov

Trust is the key to any positive human interaction, and being surrounded by trustworthy people is vitally important to the wellbeing of young people. One of the most tragic outcomes of the Royal Commission into Institutional Responses to Child Sexual Abuse was the betrayal of trust.

In a speech at the Melbourne Law School in July 2019, Banking Royal Commissioner Kenneth Hayne summed up his observations regarding the state of our society in the words, 'Trust in all sorts of institutions, governmental and private, has been damaged or destroyed.'[136] The trust deficit in our society, which has been spoken about by many commentators, was demonstrated in the 'Australia Talks' survey conducted by the national broadcaster ABC, which had 55,000 respondents. It showed that the majority of those who took the survey did not trust big business and their leaders, stating they thought big business is more about profit than what is best for Australian society, and they would exploit any situation in the name of profit.

The survey also found that trust in politicians is at a 50-year low, with 90 per cent saying they believed politicians would lie if that would help them politically, and 84 per cent saying politicians are out of touch with the people they are supposed to represent.[137]

Trust is built on respect. In the 2019 ABC Australia Talks survey, most respondents agreed that people in Australia should treat each other with more respect.[138] Respect will be regained in our society when integrity becomes a core value and people are respected, despite their differences in beliefs and outlooks.

Part III
Chapter 7: Shaping society – the personal

Be the change you want to see in the world. **Ghandi**

At present, there is a battle for the soul of the Australian people; a struggle between hope and despair, trust and distrust, truth and falsehood, fear and love, tribalism and unity. The outcome of that struggle will depend on how committed people are to change. The deterioration of the wellbeing of young people and dangers of inaction on climate change should be red flags warning of where society could be heading if no action is taken.

How is this going to happen?

Kon Karapanagiotidis gives us a clue. In 2001, after discovering people seeking asylum in Australia were living in the community with no basic support, Kon founded the Asylum Seeker Resource Centre (ASRC) in Melbourne. From humble beginnings, the ASRC is now a dynamic and compassionate organisation that supports thousands of people seeking asylum.

All his life, Kon was told he is naïve for thinking love is a triumphant force that brings out the best in people, that compassion can conquer anything and that being vulnerable is powerful. In his book *The Power of Hope*, Kon states triumphantly:

> I am here to tell you that all these things are true. Love transcends all because when we lead with it, we are at our best. In some ways this four-letter word seems radical in our current times. Love refuses to kneel at the altar of self-interest and fear, and it refuses to be seduced by that which diminishes us.[139]

Leading with the heart

Leading with love means an activated heart. The improved mental health of our young is going to depend on the number of young people willing to contribute to a society shaped by the language of the heart. The pandemic apocalyptically uncovered the raw nerve of collective pain and shattered the illusion that we operate in isolation in this world. It showed how interconnected we are and how we impact others. This impact can be negative, as was shown by an intensive-care expert who was able to demonstrate that one person infected with coronavirus can end up infecting 59,000 others in a snowball effect.[140] However, it has also been shown many times that a positive, caring individual can be like a magnet and influence others towards acts of kindness.

Polish poet Stanisław Jerzy Lec said, 'Each snowflake in an avalanche pleads not guilty.' It is now time for everyone who cares about who we are as a society, and who we wish to be going forward, needs to activate their heart. Two important contributors to helping this happen are setting an intention and calming the mind.

Setting an intention

We use compasses for our physical journey, and we also need to set our true north for how we want to operate in the world, what we think is important and where we want to expend our energy and resources. Those decisions are informed by choosing love over fear, action over inaction, hope over despair, justice over inequality, solidarity over selfishness, tolerance over hate and inclusion over exclusion. Every choice has political and social implications.

Calming the mind

Native Americans tell a story about an old Cherokee teaching his grandson about life:

> 'A fight is going on inside me,' he says to the boy. 'It is a terrible fight and it is between two wolves. One is evil – he is anger, envy, sorrow, regret, greed, arrogance, self-pity, guilt, resentment, inferiority, lies, false pride, superiority, and ego.'

> He continues, 'The other is good – he is joy, peace, love, hope, serenity, humility, kindness, benevolence, empathy, generosity, truth and compassion. The same fight is going on inside you – and inside every other person, too.'

The grandson thinks about it for a minute and then asks his grandfather: 'Which wolf will win?'

The old Cherokee simply replies, 'The one you feed.'[141]

In order to 'feed the right wolf' and translate intentions into action, we need a calm mind. Buddha once said, 'Since everything is a reflection of our minds ... everything can be changed by our minds.' The Buddhist tradition has given us a profound understanding of the mind and how we can use it to open ourselves to the wisdom of our hearts. It teaches us that a calm mind has three basic qualities: the first is our natural intelligence, an intuitive knowing what the right thing to do is in any situation; the second is our natural warmth, our shared capacity to love, show compassion and feel gratitude; the third is natural openness, which allows us to access the spaciousness of our minds. These can be accessed through practising mindfulness.

Each of us has feelings, memories, hopes, fears, sorrows and regrets, and they shape how we experience the world. Mindfulness is about developing self-awareness around how our minds work so that we are able to make choices around how we react. In order to make sense of the world, our mind accumulates and combines millions of partial truths and volumes of incomplete data to put together a somewhat cohesive pattern of reality and, based on this, makes presumptions about predictable outcomes. Physical skills such as driving, walking or playing a sport become automatic. However, through repetition, mental and emotional attitudes can also become automatic so that ingrained perceptions, emotions and attitudes shape our beliefs and attitudes towards life and establish an image of ourselves.

Through meditation – the formal practice of mindfulness – we start to see how the endless chatter of our minds reinforces the image we have developed, and we learn that it is not as solid as we thought. We focus our attention on the present moment, observing what is happening in the body and the mind at the present time. As we sit we become curious and start to notice how a simple thought can blossom into a full-blown chain reaction as we think about things happening in the present time, things that have happened in the past or things we think will happen in the future. We notice how easily we start worrying, wishing and wanting. We compare ourselves to others, judge others, criticise ourselves so that jealousy, fear, shame, envy, insecurity, embarrassment, anger, frustration, abandonment or disappointment grip us. These are our automatic responses.

However, Buddhists teach that the mind is spacious and has a deep wisdom and intelligence. It is like a blue open sky and our thoughts are merely like clouds passing. Through the intentional and repeated practise of mindfulness, we learn that we can notice them but also make a choice around how we react to them, gradually gaining mastery over our minds. This means that instead of the mind taking us anywhere it wants, we can embrace the present moment with a quiet mind free of chatter and chaos, and a heart that is open, compassionate and wise. We learn to understand that although we cannot control life, we can expand the mind so we can accommodate uncomfortable feelings as they arise. It has been said that dealing with uncomfortable feelings like this is like putting a teaspoon of salt in a large freshwater pond versus in a small glass, because thoughts come into the vast space of the mind and we do not shut down around it. Our hearts remain open.

Note: If you would like to start practising meditation, there is a simple one included in the Resources section at the back of this book.

 *The Language of Hope*

Chapter 8: Shaping society – the collective

By believing passionately in something that does not exist, we create it. The non-existent is whatever we have not sufficiently desired.
Franz Kafka

Both the 2020 devastating bushfires and the COVID-19 crisis showed that kindness and empathy for others can come naturally to Australians, and that the spirit of caring is reflected in the groups and organisations who fight for a decent, compassionate society and a healthy environment. Many of them have tried to influence the government to get the right people elected; to get good laws passed and effective policies introduced so that our society has the systems, structures and cultures that work in the best interests of all. However, they have not been able to work together enough to drive substantive political change, so inequality, social problems and environmental damage continue. We know there is a new story ready to be told.

The heart's language beckons us forward to act so we have a society that embraces a culture of kindness, which upholds the

values of fairness and equality, and a government that plans and acts for the common good rather than serving vested interests.

The action that is needed takes place in three directions:

1. **Upwards:** advocating for policy change and appropriate use of resources.
2. **Sideways:** encouraging and motivating people to take action.
3. **Downwards:** taking local action.

Shared principles and shared vision

In order to get the ball rolling, there will need to be a powerful enough vision for all the groups and people using the heart's language to want to walk in the same direction. A good place to start is to identify principles that everyone agrees on. An example of what the principles could look like include those put forward by Matt Fisher, a Senior Research Fellow with the Southgate Institute for Health, Society and Equity at Flinders University in Adelaide.[142] These are:

- **Principle 1.** The expression of many individual and corporate interests in a market economy do not necessarily add up to the common good. The state has a fundamental role to regulate market activities and use public resources to ensure the public interest.
- **Principle 2.** It is the urgent duty of the state and every citizen to address climate change and move to an ecologically sustainable society, as a matter of essential public interest.
- **Principle 3.** Human development, health and wellbeing are core public interests essential for a healthy democracy and modern economy. All Australian citizens should

have the opportunity to develop their potential, enjoy good health and live a decent life.

- **Principle 4.** Individuals and communities must be engaged in processes of creating a healthy society, within their own local regions. Although government-led policy, resources and services are crucial to protect and promote the common good, they are not enough.
- **Principle 5.** Australians should come together to support Aboriginal and Torres Strait Islander self-determination and follow the path of change and reconciliation set out in the Uluru Statement from the Heart. Aboriginal and Torres Strait Islander values of community wellbeing and care for country are important for all Australians.

When a vision is formed, it must take into account wisdom of the past, realities of the present, best hope for possibilities for the future, and embodiment through practice.

Unity

To gain real momentum, there needs to be a sense of unity. Coherence and impact only come when there is unity. During the pandemic, people have united against a common enemy: the COVID-19 virus. The time has now come for people of goodwill to work together for a common purpose.

The stumbling blocks of the past need to be identified, and there has to be a willingness to lay down the swords and work collaboratively to achieve the greater good. One of the barriers to unity has been groups just focusing on one issue rather than understanding that there is no such thing as a single issue, because we do not live in a single-issue world, and issues such as climate change, a broken democracy, economic inequality and social injustice are all interrelated. What is needed is a 'bigger we'.

Another barrier to unity has been harmoniousness. Sometimes loyalty to a party, faction or a particular ideology has led to people organising politically to advance a special interest or a set of beliefs, setting up prejudices and rigid thinking that constrains their willingness to collaborate with others, even though they may broadly want the same outcomes. This has often resulted in people being quick to judge others who think differently to themselves. Kon Karapanagiotidis has reflected on this and said:

> Do you want to have an impact, or do you just want to be right? Do you want to build a movement, or is winning more important? Do you want to inspire people to act, or do you want them to do so temporarily through shame and guilt? Do you want to affirm and engage the best in people, or do you want to feel self-righteous and judge others?
>
> We bring people with us when we show that the change we seek from them is an affirmation and re-commitment to their values and themselves, not a rejection of them. We bring people with us when we lead with our values – that is the only thing that can triumph over fear and a disregard for facts.
>
> Let's not be constantly enraged but rather informed. Let's not seek to be right but rather shape and build consensus. There is simply no point thinking you're right and getting on your pedestal, then looking down and seeing that no-one is following you or listening to you.[143]

We are not always aware of our filters and reactions because of firmly held positions. People are complex, and views are shaped by life experiences, so rushing to put a label on somebody before engaging with them can mean opportunities to learn, understand and find common ground are missed. Wisdom comes from many different places. New pathways towards collaboration and cooperation in service to the greater good can be discovered if people are willing to enter into respectful dialogue with each other and commit to listening, building relationships and respecting differences.

Grassroots power

I am telling you there is hope. I have seen it. But it does not come from governments or corporations. It comes from the people.
Greta Thunberg

Power is basically about 'who decides' – being at the table when decisions are made or being able to influence those at the table. The reality is, if people do not learn how to practise power, someone else will do it for them in their name, but often against their interests.

It is easy for ordinary citizens to feel they are powerless; however, the reality is that they have a lot more power than they realise.

Power as voters

At times, politicians have depended on the Australian population being passive, shrugging their shoulders, and averting their eyes to anything that does not directly affect them. However, as Albert Einstein once said, 'The world will not be destroyed by those who do evil but by those who watch them without doing anything.' Everything can change if enough people refuse to stay silent and become part of a #QuietNoMore movement. Injustice, stupidity or corruption can be called out, and decisions made in boardrooms and the halls of government can change.

Politicians are accountable to voters, and the one thing many politicians fear most is angry voters who want change. When voters become aware of issues and get serious about change, they are a powerful force if they are prepared to work together. One successful grassroots movement is GetUp![144] Established in 2005 as a people's movement, it aims to work towards a fair, flourishing and just society based on people, power and impact. It has a membership of over one million Australians and has attracted people who have shared values of fairness, compassion and courage. It works in the areas of environmental justice, human rights, economic fairness and democratic integrity. It takes on powerful interests and aims to hold the government to account. It has had a number of victories, including the following:

- **High Court case.** On 13 August, 2010, the GetUp! community took on the *Commonwealth Electoral Act 1918* and won! The High Court ruled that Howard-era laws that close the electoral rolls on the day that writs for an election are issued are invalid. This is because closing of the rolls disenfranchised thousands of Australians, and especially young Australians, at the 2007 election and threatened to do so again. During the seven-day enrolment period last allowed at the 2004 federal election, 423,000 people either enrolled for the first time or changed their address or other details. In 2010, the landmark announcement allowed a potential 98,138 extra people to enrol for the 2010 federal election.
- **Election campaign.** During the 2010 federal election, GetUp! members made it possible to flood the airwaves

100

with ads on a variety of issues, including climate change policy, refugees and asylum seeker policy, mental health funding and gender equality. Over 7,000 volunteers helped carry out this major campaign. GetUp! members were more generous than they had ever been before in chipping in to make sure these ads were on the air in the lead-up to election day.

- **Mental health campaign.** GetUp! launched a campaign in 2010 aiming to bring awareness around the need for increased funding for mental health. Support for the campaign exploded, resulting in the community retrieving 104,641 signatures in support of the campaign, and a candlelit statement sprawled across the lawn of Parliament House. In a huge community success, an extra $2.2 billion was awarded towards mental health in the 2011 federal budget.

- **Great Barrier Reef under threat.** When news came to light that one of our national icons may be under threat, GetUp! members rallied together and a petition containing an astounding 101,935 signatures was lodged with UNESCO. This petition was highly influential in Russia at the World Heritage Committee meeting, as shown by the passing of recommendations calling on the Australian Government to take action by 1 February, 2013. The petition to defend the Barrier Reef grew to over 120,000 signatures before being presented to the Minister for the Environment at the time, Tony Burke.

- **Equal before the law.** 2007 saw the beginning of GetUp!'s push towards equal rights for all members of the community, regardless of their sexual orientation. Wide media coverage of GetUp's poll indicated that over 70 per cent of Australians believed that same-sex couples should be given legal equality in de facto relationships.

The GetUp! community rallied together, with 26,000 members signing a petition to this effect. Despite these efforts, the government did not amend the bill. Unphased, the community only grew stronger and the petition gained support, rapidly reaching 50,000 signatures. By November 2008, the Senate finally took note. It removed the laws discriminating against same-sex couples and gave all Australians equal rights in de facto relationships, regardless of their sexual orientation.

- **Bank on it.** The GetUp! community joined forces with the well-known and regarded Australian organisation Choice to take a stand against bank fees. As a community they fought to remove penalty fees and excessive margins on mortgage rates. The campaign aimed to encourage 'greater social responsibility by business and corporations'. To achieve this outcome, the GetUp! community, in conjunction with Choice, backed a class action lawsuit against ANZ. The lawsuit aimed to retrieve $50 million in late fees paid by 27,000 ANZ members over the previous six years.

- **Sorry is the first step.** Over 40,000 GetUp! members rallied together to encourage the government to 'say sorry' to Australia's Indigenous community. The movement saw a moving candlelit arrangement of the message 'Sorry is the first step' laid out across the front lawn of Canberra's Parliament House. This symbolic message was reinforced with thousands of GetUp! members attending over 350 'Reconciliation Get Togethers' in public halls, living rooms and campfires across the nation.

- **Ban live exports campaign.** After a *Four Corners* episode on live exports shocked the nation, the GetUp! community came together and provided a quarter of a million signatures calling for the ban of live exports –

making it GetUp!'s largest and fastest-growing petition ever. It was presented to Parliament House in a press conference with the RSPCA, Animals Australia and the Australasian Meat Industry Employees Union (AMIEU). As a result, Julia Gillard immediately suspended live exports to Indonesia.[145]

When individual members of society work together at a grassroots level to bring about change, they tap into what Jeremy Heimans and Henry Timms explore in their book *New Power*, which is the difference between Old Power and New Power. Old Power is the dominant power operating in our society at present. It is like a currency held in the hands of those in government and is difficult to challenge. Once gained, this power is jealously guarded because there is a substantial store to spend. It is downloaded from the top and is enabled by people and organisations who have a good understanding of how it can be controlled. It is formal and institutional, and its message to the general public is 'comply, pay your taxes, do your homework, and consume'.[146]

New Power operates differently. It is informal, networked and it is in the hands of many. It is like a current, open, participatory, collaborative and peer-driven system, and it reinforces the human instinct to cooperate. It is like water – uploading and distributing – and is most powerful when it surges. It tends to be decentralised, grassroots-driven, non-partisan, inclusive, non-violent and mission-focused. Supported by the internet, it has opened up new ways of communicating, participating and taking action. It is ambitious, creative and is open to sharing new ideas and creating new content.[147]

When New Power finds its voice, it can be confronting to Old Power. In September 2019, when Greta Thunberg mobilised millions of people around the world in climate strikes, there was a strong reaction from the warriors of Old Power. Alan Jones, conservative Sydney radio host stated that she and her followers were 'badly educated virtue-signalling turds',[148] while Sam Newman, a TV sports commentator, called her an 'annoying little brat'.[149] *Herald Sun* columnist Andrew Bolt joined in the general chorus of abuse and stated she was 'deeply disturbed'.[150]

Irish journalist Jennifer O'Connell asked, 'Why is Greta Thunberg so triggering to certain men?' She concluded that it was because of what she represents: 'the emergence of a new kind of power, a convergence of youth, popular protest and irrefutable science'.[151]

Power as consumers

Corporations are multinational or national bodies set up to produce or deliver a product or service and deliver maximum profits to their shareholders. A corporation may pay lobbyists to influence government to make decisions that often promote the interests of the corporation, with little regard for their social and environmental impact. As their behaviour and decisions have been scrutinised, trust in corporations has diminished, and corporate leaders are starting to realise that lack of trust affects their bottom line. The Price Waterhouse 20th CEO Survey found that two-thirds of Australian CEOs were concerned about lack of trust. The growing realisation that they need to focus on what customers and shareholders see as 'doing the right thing' means that both customers and shareholders can have a lot of influence.[152]

One powerful way that customers can influence is through their buying choices, which can be an active expression of their ideals and ethics and what they value most; for example, they may show they are committed to integrity over price and convenience. Millennials are leading this area with 80 per cent stating, in a survey conducted by Deloitte Access Economics, that impact on society and the environment should be as important as financial performance when measuring the success of a product. Three out of four said they were willing to pay more for ethical and sustainable products.[153] Findings like this have led to a ripple effect across industries as diverse as fashion, food and banking.

Another growing phenomenon, called 'woke capitalism',[154] has meant that corporations are starting to redirect some of their marketing and public relations to progressive social causes, which they believe can improve their image. In Australia, Qantas took a strong position on marriage equality, and Gillette supported the #MeToo movement.

During the bushfire disaster in 2020, Tiffany & Co., a luxury jewellery company, placed a full-page statement in newspapers in capital cities demanding the government take action on climate change. They stated, 'We stand with Australia' because they sensed a shift in mainstream thinking around the need for action on climate change.[155] During that period, other companies, noticing the dissatisfaction with the bumbling response of the government, stepped up so that they would be seen to be doing the right thing. The National Bank of Australia, for example, offered $2,000 to customers who lost their homes. Woolworths and Coles delivered water and food to evacuation centres, and Qantas pledged one million dollars to bushfire relief. Optus and Telstra took care of firefighters' mobile phone bills.[156]

One of the key motivations for the purchase of luxury goods and services is to display status. Marketers spend a lot of money and energy telling consumers what a wealthy lifestyle looks like and what they need to display to show success in the social comparison stakes. The purchase of goods that are rare is one way a person can show status differentiation. In May 2019, an Intergovernmental Science-Policy Platform on Biodiversity and

Ecosystem Services (IPBES) report confirmed one million species are potentially facing extinction. As a species becomes rare, it becomes valuable. Some of the most endangered species in the world are legally traded in the most lucrative and exclusive industries. According to a 2018 report on luxury goods by Bain & Company, the overall luxury market grew five per cent in 2018, to an estimated US $1.32 trillion. Endangered species contribute to value in the luxury market through:

- personal luxury (clothing, accessories, jewellery, beauty, wellbeing, etc.)
- high-end furniture and housewares
- luxury hospitality, fine dining and gourmet food
- the exotic pet industry (from parrots and reptiles to big cats)
- trophy hunting and other luxury travel.

Sometimes, the trade tips into an illegal trade when there is a demand. For example, fennec foxes in the wake of the release of Disney's *Zootopia*, or the recent trend of having otters available to cuddle in some of Japan's cafés.

In order to find an alternative way for elites to fulfil their self-image needs and 'win' in the social comparison stakes, the organisation Nature Needs More has been researching a way of re-inventing 'magnificence', a concept steeped in history but subverted by luxury in recent centuries. In the past, magnificence allowed wealthy individuals to show their status and prestige and establish their social differentiation by donating large expenditures for the public good, such as constructing buildings or establishing beautiful parks. Nature Needs More believes the new magnificence could be a motivation to contribute to the natural world rather than consume its 'products'.[157]

Shareholders can exert power on corporations by the way they vote at shareholder meetings. Concerns about climate change have led to a growing number of shareholders demanding that companies become more accountable and change behaviours, if necessary.[158]

Power as communities

In 2017, the Future of Local Government Conference was held in Melbourne. It was attended by local government councillors and CEOs from all around Australia. At the summit, a strong declaration was made about the need for communities to be given more responsibility. Below is an excerpt:[159]

The need for change

This declaration rests on a belief that the state of the nation and the health of our society depends on community-driven action in the neighbourhood, not just decisions made in parliaments or boardrooms.

Across the world people are concerned about the apparent inability of governments, business and public institutions to address the economic, social and environmental challenges of the 21st Century. Our present ways of thinking and governing are neither coping with the pace of change nor meeting citizens' expectations. There is an urgent need for a fresh approach and responsive leadership.

… It's time to explore a new model of governance, one based on a re-energised civil society that draws on the strength and resourcefulness of people working together in diverse local and regional communities – a localist response.

… In this way, we can create a 'New Story' – a narrative of change built on the strengths and uniqueness of each community and place. Local government can provide the foundations for change. It can lead the process of transformation through good governance and sound administration, reinvigorating faith in democracy and citizenship. It can facilitate new forms of community-centred, bottom-up governance that inspire the confidence and active participation of citizens. It can unleash community resources and help ensure our future wellbeing.

As leaders in local government, it was suggested that councils should:

- 'Empower citizens through participatory and deliberative democracy, including community boards, precinct committees, cooperatives, citizen juries and others.
- Learn how to be community led, making space for communities to take action themselves and responding positively to local initiatives.
- Embrace new ways of working to ensure that local needs are met through joined-up planning and services.
- Promote local networks, co-production of goods and services, and moves to 'reclaim the Commons'.
- Deepen their understanding of communities, listening to all their people and engaging with them in new and different ways that reflect community diversity ...'

Note: If you would like to reflect on your own journey of change, there is an exercise on self-reflection in the Resources section at the back of this book.

Observations from yours truly, a Youth

Ciara M. Symons

The idea of hope is laughable; I know. I've jeered at it many times before. I mean, it's a four-letter word plopped into any and every adventure story – whether a movie, novel or picture book. It's overused in every instance. But that's the golden hue of childhood hope; twisting the narrative toward a joyous ending despite it being highly unbelievable.

I've scoffed at hope consistently – because it has a sickly sense of false optimism about it.

I've scoffed at hope consistently – but it's time I changed that.

Because not all hope is so sickly sweet and naive. We can have a balanced hope.

We must save the young Socrates that is within us all. And, we must allow ourselves to hope again. If we are rational, if we plan and act, if we put aside differences, we can achieve more. We can finally achieve balance. But it is dependent on a lot of ifs. **Ifs** *are no guarantees.* **Ifs** *require hard work.*

Chapter 9: Shaping society – ripples of hope

It is not the critic who counts; not the man who points out how the strong man stumbles, or where the doer of deeds could have done them better. The credit belongs to the man who is actually in the arena, whose face is marred by dust and sweat and blood; who strives valiantly; who errs … who at the best knows in the end the triumph of high achievement, and who at worst, if he fails, at least fails while daring greatly.
Theodore Roosevelt

Robert Kennedy once said, 'Each time a man stands up for an ideal, or acts to improve the lot of others, or strikes out against injustice, he sends forth a tiny ripple of hope.'[160] There is a big difference between thinking something should happen and trying to make it happen. We can protest, we can talk, but the hard work begins when an idea moves through our heads, into our hearts and then into our hands, and action is taken. The Asaro tribe of Papua New Guinea have a beautiful saying: 'Knowledge is only a rumour until it lives in the muscle.'[161]

The following Australians have shown real leadership by using their skills to translate their dreams in both social and environmental spheres to drive projects that make a real difference. With perseverance and courage, they have shown leadership by using their skills to translate dreams into projects of value. They have challenged the status quo and embodied the heart's language by giving hope, showing empathy, creating trust and fostering respectful relationships.

Marg's story

The Gandhi Experiment

Too many people are experimenting with war and violence. We need more people experimenting with peace and nonviolence. **Margaret Hepworth**

Marg Hepworth has been an educator for much of her life. Her teaching career includes time as Head of House at Caulfield Grammar and Head of Campus at Preshil School in Melbourne. In recent years, Marg has left mainstream teaching and dedicated herself to being a 'peace educator'. The seed for this decision was planted in 2000 when she was teaching at an international school in Nanjing, China, and two of her students and their parents were brutally murdered by four young men from a nearby village. This terrible incident shocked Marg into thinking about the causes of violence.

In 2010, while participating in a 'smoke ceremony' at an Indigenous studies conference at Wesley College, Marg experienced a profound moment of knowingness that she needed to *take action*. In 2014, while meditating at Sabarmati Ashram in Ahmedabad, the site of Gandhi's second ashram, that action became clear. She decided it was time to set up an initiative, which she would call 'The Gandhi Experiment'. The initiative would involve presenting workshops in schools to raise the awareness of young people about making choices around violence and non-violence in order to help them to become conscious global citizens. The workshops would focus on the main tenets of Gandhi's vision:

- Use nonviolence as a conscious choice
- 'Satyagraha' – holding onto truth or soul force
- Understanding that when my truth does not meet your truth, we never use violence as an answer
- Acting on injustice by moving from apathy to action
- Change begins with me
- My life is my message
- I will live through my values

Marg has now delivered many workshops in schools, at conferences and organisations across India, Pakistan, Indonesia, Fiji, China and Australia. She has found most young people are altruistic and want to take action but often feel overwhelmed and powerless. In her workshops she teaches them how they can have agency by accessing processes such as 'positive reality'; a phrase she coined, and where we give ourselves permission to have 'almost impossible thoughts'. She teaches her students that if they recognise a problem, they can name it and shift to a place where they can take some kind of positive action, even if it is only a small action. Feedback from students in her workshops shows that they have responded well; for example:

'I felt a newfound joy and encouragement after the session. It was very motivational. It made me realise I can change the world with my ideas and dreams for the world.'

'I was really unenthusiastic about today, but as I got into the day, I saw a totally new perspective on the day. It was so inspiring, and I really feel like I can do something in this world to help.'

'Action is when someone takes responsibility and decides to begin to make a difference and fight for what they want without helplessly sitting and whining about what is possible, never doing anything about it.'

It has not been an easy journey and there have been financial pressures, but feedback in emails from young people has been positive, such as one young Australian–Palestinian girl who attended her workshop, and said:

I would like to tell you some things I have taken away, because your seminar completely changed my outlook on things

You talked about anger, about revenge, and about forgiveness … I used to think I could never forgive them for taking the life of my family members, for how they treat us in checkpoints, for how hard they make it for us to live there, in a country that was ours before them. And yet, in the space of a day, you changed my Mind.

You spoke about Malala, and how she wished education for the Taliban's children, and how she stated that she would be no better than them if she responded without peace. You spoke about Nelson Mandela and how he forgave the people who put him in jail because harbouring hate and wanting revenge is not the way to make a change.

So that got me thinking. My impossible thought was the liberation of Palestine with punishments to the Israelis for all they have done to us. Sure, they might have pulled out couches and watched Gaza get bombed – many of them did this. BUT. If I did the same, I am no better than them, whether I have a right to revenge or not.

A deep sense of spirituality informs Marg's work. She was raised a Roman Catholic but now finds herself drawn to other spiritualities. Her connection with the Hindu Goddess Kali is profoundly important to her, bringing her 'ferocious courage'. In her workshops she explores different aspects of body, mind and spirit. She believes there needs to be a balance between heart and head because without the mind there is no logic or reason, but without the heart there is no compassion.

Marg has discovered that her message for peace resonates with people from all countries, and she is now working with teachers. These are the emails Marg sent me when she was doing teacher training in China in both 2018 and 2019.

Having a grand time in China with the teacher training. The human spirit is well and truly alive here. Today I trained 100 teachers. I had them meditating, doing role-plays, learning about positive education and much more. They told me they really appreciated learning about positive education and global citizenship. At the end of the day, I taught them a song sung by a Jewish rap artist. The song is called 'One Day' – about no more hatred / no more wars. It was really special to hear Chinese teachers singing this with such passion.

In my workshop with 16 Chinese professors from Shihezi University, the special moment came when in our final workshop, 'Almost Impossible Thoughts', each professor, all from science backgrounds, stood up to share what they would be taking home. They spoke of how they had come to a sense of shared global humanity, giving very specific examples of how they would develop their own research projects to help shape a more positive future for all.

115

In 2015, after taking her workshops across India, Marg returned home to Melbourne to discover a letter in her inbox asking if she would write her workshop into a book. Thinking it was spam, Marg almost pressed 'delete'. Fortunately, she didn't and responded to the request from Rupa Publications. Subsequently, *The Gandhi Experiment – Teaching our teenagers how to become global citizens* was published in 2017. She has also authored the books *Collaborative Debating* and *Clarity in Time*. She is the recipient of the Sir John Monash Award for Inspirational Women's Leadership 2016, and the 2019 India Australia Business and Community Awards for Community Services Excellence.

Shakti's story

The Hills Food Frontier (THFF)

Shakti McLaren lives in the Dandenong Ranges, Victoria. Shakti is passionate about sustainability, the importance of food security and communities growing their own food. She believes that this will enable them to control their own destinies. Ultimately, she would like to see vibrant good-food projects such as THFF well-funded by the government.

In 2014, Shakti, with a group of likeminded individuals, initiated The Hills Food Frontier, which is a 'food revolution' project that promotes and facilitates the growing and sharing of nutritious, wholesome, affordable food within the Dandenong Ranges. They want to see the region become an inspirational, sustainable food destination. THFF is built on values such as ethical care for the environment, inclusivity, social justice and compassion. They have worked tirelessly to achieve the following objectives:

- **Good food growing**: by supporting and developing food gardens and forests in the community, engaging schools, businesses, local community, residents, and accessing unused land and utilising creative spaces.
- **Good food eating**: by promoting local good food cafés and restaurants, sharing what good food activities already exist, developing and facilitating gatherings/ festivals, demonstrations, and including local businesses.
- **Good food promotion**: by using social media, their website, flyers, noticeboards, word of mouth, networking, newsletters, presentations and the local media.
- **Good food learning**: by developing and promoting educational sessions and resources focused on growing and eating.

THFF collaborated with the local Uniting Church, which has generously given the group ongoing access to their building and land around church buildings. THFF has also been strongly supported by community members and groups, such as the Bendigo Bank and the local Rotary Club as well as their local council and state government members. The group has worked as a team, who build on the strengths of their members rather than setting up a hierarchical structure.

Outcomes:

- **The FLAME Garden.** THFF has established a vibrant community garden, which they have called the FLAME Garden, which embraces Food, Life, Art, Music and Education. The garden contains a food forest, fresh vegetables, fruit trees, compost, artwork by a local student describing aspects of the garden, and a worm farm. Wicking beds, a pollination garden and a tea garden have also been established.

They have named the path leading to the garden of yam daisies, chocolate lilies and native grass 'It's Thyme for Reconciliation Pathway'. The path has a wattle tree on one side, a symbol of Australia, and a 'thyme wall' on the other. The natural sculptured artworks placed beside the path symbolise open arms and reaching for the heavens.

The garden has provided great opportunities for all members of the community to grow food, learn new skills and develop new friendships. It welcomes people from diverse and different backgrounds, including the young and elderly. A garden flower fence with different art installations has been incorporated into the garden to add colour and vibrancy.

Workshops have been provided on such topics as:
- composting
- bee keeping
- mushroom log growing
- permaculture.

- **Food is Free Tecoma (FIFT).** The tremendous generosity of spirit of THFF and their community is captured in the Food is Free Tecoma (FIFT) initiative. A cupboard and fridge are provided, and people are invited to take and give food. It is open to the whole community.
- **Food security network program.** In 2018 and '19, a Food Security Network Program was implemented at the local Upwey High School and Sassafras Primary School. Both schools had successful harvests, which they gave to FIFT and the Asylum Seeker Resource Centre in Footscray.
- **The Hills Edible Villages (HEV) project.** In 2019, THFF expanded to a neighbouring community in Kallista where the Edible Kallista Action Group was formed. It meets regularly for shared dinners and is working on a community planting project.

Donalea's story

For the Love of Wildlife

For the Love of Wildlife is about restoring the essential connection between all living things to bring the planet into balance.

Donalea Patman founded For the Love of Wildlife Ltd. in early 2014 as a professional platform to campaign the plight of wildlife and to raise awareness of the destructive forces annihilating the natural world. In recognition of the great contribution she has made in the area of animal welfare, Donalea was the recipient of the Animal Action Award, International Fund for Animal Welfare (IFAW) and was awarded an Order of Australia Medal in 2017.

Her inspiration came from when she was with Andrew Harvey at a workshop on Sacred Activism in Timbavati, South Africa. She describes it here:

> The very first morning, we all gathered well before dawn, headlamps on and ready to climb aboard the open jeeps to see if we could see lions. It was just on sunrise when we turned a corner and surprised a pride who sat up at the sudden arrival with one of the sub-adult males locking eyes with me. Despite being told not to lock eyes with a lion, I couldn't help myself, I was transfixed, and the pure emotion welled up and I quietly sobbed; this moment would change my life forever. I couldn't quite believe that lions could be so magnificent, hold such an incredible field; they are simply exquisite.

> Back at camp a few hours later, I was told about the plight of wild lions and heard for the very first time the hideous and abhorrent industry of captive breeding and

canned hunting. I was so enraged, a feeling I had never experienced before, a primal searing rage and I asked Andrew what to do with this energy as I sat there in my distress and the discomfort of this unfamiliar feeling. Andrew looked at me and said, 'Now that you've been brought to your knees in your indignant rage, your despair and your grief for the plight of lions, I want you to transform this energy through your passionate heart and go out into the world and do something about it!' You can't remain the same after an experience like that and this was part of the transformation that led me to the work I find myself in now.

Donalea has always had a deep love for animals, and she is a passionate advocate for sentient beings. She has travelled extensively throughout her life, with the most defining and memorable moments always involving animals. Even as a small girl she remembers telling her father and his friend that riding turtles off a remote beach in Western Australia was 'interfering with nature!'

With background in corporate business and more than 25 years' experience in corporate communications for both Australian and international companies, Donalea is now a company director, practising designer, animal advocate and lead figure working with the Australian Government addressing the plight of wildlife. She achieved a global first with Australia banning the importation of lion trophies and body parts – a direct response to the cruel and barbaric industry of canned hunting, where lions are bred for the bullet.

This work went on to address the rampant, unregulated domestic trade in ivory and rhino horn in Australia, hosting Australia's first ivory and rhino horn crush event on World Wildlife Day 2018 in Melbourne. This gained international press coverage and triggered a Parliamentary Inquiry on Law Enforcement, with Australia announcing it would enact a ban in Geneva, August 2019, at the Conference on the International Trade in Endangered Species in Wild Flora and Fauna (CITES). This domestic trade ban is yet to be enacted by the Australian states. The investigations exposed that the legal trade in endangered species is unfit for purpose and has not been updated since the '70s. For the Love of Wildlife, working with Nature Needs More, have met with more than 30 signatory countries in a proposal to modernise the trade, which, as it stands, allows the illegal trade to be easily laundered through it.

Clare's story

Kindred Kindness

Clare Pritchard is a yoga teacher who trained initially in the Iyengar method and has gone on to focus on Trauma Sensitive Yoga in her clinical work with survivors. She believes that a yoga practice is an opportunity to find stillness, and strength, and a base from which to connect with and care for both self and others. Clare has two children and she has experienced many of the joys and challenges associated with motherhood. Clare has been one of the driving forces behind a small but dynamic group called Kindred Kindness. Kindred was formed in 2014 by a group of likeminded women from the Dandenong Ranges who were deeply concerned about the federal government's asylum seeker policies and how they reflected the society that their children were going to grow up in.

Clare was motivated to step into a space where she could support people seeking asylum and to join with others to try to make a difference there because she was appalled by the punitive and cruel government policies relating to asylum seekers arriving in Australia. These policies were and are particularly inhumane in the way in which those who arrive by boat are treated (and mistreated), but a long campaign of 'othering' by both politicians and media has ensured that public attitude towards refugees is primarily grounded in fear and mistrust. The vision of Kindred is reflected in the following statement from their website:

> The organisation envisages a kinder and more compassionate Australia, where communities are empowered to work together in welcoming Asylum Seekers. By forming friendships with people seeking asylum, it aims to welcome them with compassion and assist them in accessing support services and integrating into the community. Through the sharing of common humanity and celebrating our cultural differences, the organisation aims to build a more compassionate world through simple acts of kindness.

In the beginning, part of Kindred's primary focus was visiting people held in the detention centre in Broadmeadows (MITA) and simply offering them friendship and support. In time, many of these individuals and families have been moved on – into the community, onto visas, or into offshore detention centres – and Kindred members have tried to maintain contact and offer continued support.

Kindred has also focused on community engagement, through material aid collections, fundraising events, vigils and more. It has a significant Facebook presence in the Dandenong Ranges, and this support base extends right across Melbourne.

Clare's reflection on what is useful in taking socio-political action is, 'Be brave, take action – even a small action; speak up; find others who share your beliefs and passion; look after yourself, pace yourself; take time to regularly reflect on what you do.' She admits there are challenges in taking action. It is difficult and impacting to be exposed to such extreme human suffering and to sit with feeling hopeless and powerless to make real, effective change. She describes feelings of enormous guilt – for having been so lucky to win the 'global lottery of privilege', and for feeling unable to ever do enough.

Other challenges include dealing with group dynamics and balancing activism with work/family demands. However, she is sustained in times of difficulty and disappointment by the strength of the human connection between the brave and resilient people that Kindred supports, and the many dedicated and strong people who stand beside them.

On the heart's language, her reflections are:

- **Hope**. We are in a great position of responsibility to hold onto hope for those who have lost it. Just by sharing a moment, by **seeing** someone who has been made invisible, by **listening** to someone who has been silenced, we can provide hope.
- **Empathy**. Trying to understand another person's suffering is a great driver in choosing to help and support, hear and see them.
- **Action**. It is so important in feeling a sense of empowerment. Inaction changes nothing and only feeds feelings of guilt/shame.
- **Relationships**. This is the most powerful way to break down concepts of the 'other', realising we are all the same at some level. Working together provides strength, support, energy.
- **Trust**. Digging deep to trust that things can (and will?) get better.

Judy's story

Three Sides of the Coin: using theatre to create change

When we own the story, we can write a brave new ending. **Brené Brown**

Judy Avisar is driven by a desire for social justice, believing that without fairness, there can be no wellness in society. Her awareness of inequality was awakened early in life when she contrasted her affluent lifestyle to some of her classmates whose families were struggling.

She feels we live in a *me* culture where it is all about *my* rights, *my* benefits, *my* growth; an approach that can become very narcissistic. In contrast, in a *we* culture we can begin thinking about the greater whole and the greater good, bringing together the individual and the community, psychology and politics, in an endeavour to engender change.

Judy's background is in community development. She works with people who have been personally harmed by gambling, people who are prepared to be vulnerable and brave to face their own demons and advocate for change in our society. Judy coordinates the Three Sides of the Coin project, an innovative and creative approach to raising awareness of gambling harm through storytelling and theatre.

Participants can be people who have gambled themselves or people who have suffered due to the gambling of someone close to them. Creative workshops give participants a chance to meet others in similar situations, to tell their stories in a safe, non-judgemental space. They gain confidence and develop trust and connection with themselves and other group members.

With authenticity and courage, they share the inner voices, the pain, the shame, the harm of it all, and gain strength to journey on the path of self-discovery to recovery.

Under the sensitive guidance of artistic director Catherine Simmonds, performance scenes are created through weaving people's personal stories into a creative whole, so they can be performed publicly, revealing the shame and stigma of gambling, as well as how its normalisation harms our communities. Audiences are impacted emotionally and viscerally, and Three Sides of the Coin can begin to change the community conversation around gambling. Professionals in allied fields of mental health, alcohol and drugs, and family violence begin to understand the often hidden links to gambling, and are encouraged to include gambling in their conversations with clients.

> *The people at the Three Sides of the Coin project have shown more courage and bravery than I've ever seen. Their commitment to telling their painful story to help others overcome their own challenges shows enormous compassion and determination. And the manner in which they tell the story has made me laugh and cry concurrently.* **Serge Sardo, former CEO of the Victorian Responsible Gambling Foundation**

> *We learn much more than just how to 'perform our lives'; we learn about creativity, the power of listening to ourselves and others; hearing voices other than the dark shaming ones we have lived with for so many years. We offer the unique support of the lived experience to each other. We see how our stories are woven together to make a whole that helps audiences better understand gambling addiction and recovery.* **Participant**

> *To witness these scenes is to witness the truth – it bypasses your brain and touches your heart.* **Audience member**

Lea's story

The Liora Project; Guria; Woman and Child Health Project, Jagriti Bhalai Kendra Society; Connecting Conversations.

Lea Trafford is a dynamic woman with broad horizons. She is passionate about empowering women both overseas and here in Australia. She is involved with a number of heart-driven projects in India as well as one she has created here in Australia.

The Liora Project

Lea is a board member of The Liora Project (a registered Australian charity), which supports women and children who are living in abject poverty in the central-western area of India, particularly women and their children who have been trafficked into the sex industry.

In this project, women are transitioned into new lives by being given education and training so that they have an alternate means of earning an income. Currently, the project manages two sewing training centres, which employ many of the women, and the organisation is working to create a centre to care for the varied needs of their children. A strong focus for Lea is raising funds for these initiatives and also raising awareness around the worldwide human trafficking trade.

Guria

As an indirect consequence of her involvement with The Liora Project, Lea is also connected to an NGO, Guria, in Varanasi, India, which was created to prevent child prostitution and the trafficking of women and children. It has established a number of schools with the view to eliminating second-generation prostitution through education, and care of all the children.

Lea has become a supporter/funder/producer for a new documentary to enable the story of this remarkable work to be told.

Woman and Child Health Project, Jagriti Bhalai Kendra Society

Lea is involved in the ongoing support of the Woman and Child Health Project, Jagriti Bhalai Kendra Society, which was created by Dr Alma Ram. This project walks alongside women in the villages of the Punjab region in North India. Established in 2010, the project aims to address health, social and environmental issues. The focus to date has been on nutrition, female empowerment, gender equality, contraception, all issues associated with HIV/Aids, and assisting with access to government initiatives. Education is also provided to both men and women in their villages with an aim to preventing STIs and HIV, to highlight the dangers of female foeticide and conversations with regards to the practices of honour killing. The project is for the benefit of all castes, creeds and religions – with a special focus on the Dalit (untouchables) communities. Lea's specific interest and involvement is in sustainability and the empowerment of women to create their own earning power.

Lea reacts to what she calls the 'charity model' of helping vulnerable people. She has observed that this often results in doing things to, and for, people, rather than *with* people. She has discovered that whatever their circumstances, people have something to offer and want to be appreciated for who they are. Her wide range of experiences and interactions has made her see that there are common themes in everybody's lives, and that when people listen to each other deeply, and are prepared to share their vulnerabilities, they can have a lot to share.

Connecting Conversations

These understandings led Lea to create the Connecting Conversations project in Australia. She wanted to create environments where people could form deep connections and have meaningful conversations. Many people will resonate with what Lea sees as a 'connecting conversation':

> To listen is to understand. To understand is to have compassion.

> We have all experienced conversations that are disconnecting from ourselves and the other.

> When we come together for the joy of listening to and hearing others, we can connect at a deep level.

> So often we are more concerned with being heard than hearing what the other has to say.

> Connecting Conversations is about listening to the other for meaning and understanding.

> They invite us to be willing to stand in a place that is unknown and maybe a little uncomfortable.

> They are an invitation to be Curious, to be Present, to be Available and to Deeply Listen.

Since its inception in 2016, Lea has created situations where women only (so far) can experience this opportunity. They are invited to a small one-off event for a shared meal and conversation around a selected word or topic. They are asked to hold the word or topic loosely, to listen deeply (without feedback), notice any judgements that may arise, and to hold space for all opinions. They are invited to bring their curiosity and an open heart and notice similarities rather than differences.

Lea now also facilitates Women's Circles, for women who have been curious enough to attend one of the Connecting Conversations shared meals and have chosen to attend regular monthly gatherings for taking the conversation even deeper.

Belinda's story

Tribe-Monbulk Youth Inc.

Belinda Grooby is a woman of passion and drive who cares deeply about young people. She is a mother of teenage children so is well aware of the challenges faced by young people in today's society. As a resident of Monbulk, a small town in Victoria, she has become increasingly concerned over the years about the lack of opportunities for young teens to connect with each other and their community outside of school and sport.

In order to address the problem, Belinda launched Tribe, an independent, non-religious group for young people aged between 13–17 in April 2018. The motto of the group was 'Be yourself, join our Tribe'. It was an instant success, and in 2019 she started another group for children aged 8–12. The group met on Friday nights and by 2020 it was supporting over 70 young people. Belinda's desire for inclusivity led to young people with disabilities and those from non-English-speaking backgrounds being embraced by the group.

The group is totally youth focused, and the young people themselves decide how they will work together. Youth-led committees make decisions regarding group and fundraising activities. The group has no agenda other than to provide a safe space for young people to connect with each other, have fun and to talk about issues that are important to them. The only non-negotiable is 'no drugs, alcohol or smoking'.

129

In addition to the weekly sessions, there are regular outings and excursions, such as roller skating, cinema, African drumming, laser tag, and even trips to the snow.

Volunteer staff provide guidance on money handling, conflict resolution, team building etc. There have been workshops on 'how to adult', and pathways to employment. Some of the original members, now too old to be in the group itself, have returned as volunteers to help with younger children. The group works with local mental health agencies to address any wellbeing issues that may arise.

The group is well supported by the community. The increased wellbeing and prosocial behaviour of the participants have been noticed and appreciated by parents, schools, police and the general community. Belinda's work has also been positively recognised by the Yarra Ranges Council with an Australia Day Award for outstanding dedication to the community.

The websites of all the projects in this section are in the Resources section at the end of the book.

A call to action

Fight for the things that you care about but do it in a way that will lead others to join you. **Ruth Bader Ginsburg**

On Sunday, 2 September, 1666, a fire broke out in a bakery in London. At that time, open flames were used for heat, light and cooking. The fire spread with savage intensity through the city where most of the buildings were built of wood and thatch and were pressed close together. The inferno raged for four days and the fire – now known as The Great Fire of London – destroyed the homes of 70,000 out of the 80,000 inhabitants of the city. All that was left in the aftermath was a question... How do we rebuild? The old way clearly did not work.

Pre-COVID-19

Well before the COVID-19 pandemic, many people questioned the direction of society and tried to change things. Young people marched in the streets pleading with the government to take the warnings of scientists seriously. However, just as in London before the fire, our leaders just kept doing 'business as usual', unwittingly creating a society that worked against everything that nourishes and supports societal wellbeing.

We lived in a society where fierce competition and individualism were the building blocks. As we focused on profit

at any cost; greed, suspicion and selfishness became the norm. It was a society where protecting the environment and living in harmony with nature were not seen as important as the bottom line. Even though scientists continually warned us about the danger of not taking action on climate change, those in power brushed that knowledge away because power and money were up for grabs. It was a society where the tears in the social fabric were becoming more and more apparent and trust and respect were fading. We put some nice paint on the façade of our society, but the foundations were starting to rot, and our young people knew it. Their despair was revealed in the growing statistics around their deteriorating mental health, but it was a slow burn and society just kept going.

COVID-19

Then came COVID-19 – an apocalyptic shakeup – which showed us how fragile the society we have built really is. The invisible and deadly virus caused havoc, and our society was in tatters. Research showed that young people were disproportionately affected by the mental health tsunami that engulfed the population. It was time to ask the same question asked in London all those years ago. How do we rebuild?

Possible Post-COVID-19 future

Albert Einstein is credited as saying, '*The definition of insanity is doing the same thing over and over again and expecting a different result.*'

When London was to be rebuilt it was clear there had to be decisions around building materials and safety. Authorities listened to the experts. Limits were placed on proximity between buildings. Wood and thatch were outlawed in favour of brick and stone. Hydrants were introduced to make water more accessible, and every area was stocked with fire safety equipment. The first fire brigades were formed.

The pandemic has caused many people to reflect on the society we have created in Australia and imagine how we could do things differently. During the pandemic, most people have found their relationships with others have become one of the most meaningful things in their lives. Kindness has emerged in many different nooks and crannies, and local communities have taken on a new significance. People have come to realise the value of cooperation, collaboration, kindness, respect, innovation and inclusion, and asked if these were the right building materials to build a stronger, more cohesive society. Both the bushfires and the COVID-19 crisis showed these values were in society in abundance. The question is, how can they become the materials of choice as we rebuild our society?

After the Great Fire, a better and more beautiful London blossomed from the ashes. Stunning feats of art and architecture, such as the new St Paul's Cathedral, still stand today as monuments to the power of opportunity.

Hope is being able to see light despite there being darkness. The pain that young people feel is not only theirs; it is ours as a society. The heart's language invites us to dream together and work with our young people to create a world we can believe in and in which they can thrive.

Observations from yours truly, a Youth

Ciara M. Symons

So, we must take a deep breath,

and get the ball rolling.

We shall direct ourselves in a series of steady but small increments. So small that we will feel like Sisyphus shouldering his boulder up a hill. We will feel like we are trying to cradle a candle in a blizzard. Inevitably, we will feel the dread of that one sentence we've heard over and over, weighing us down: 'It is impossible.'

But

bit by bit,

we can bear it.

Because change begins with the unseen. It is the kind of change that happens within one's mind – it is the desire to act. SO, LET US TAKE ACTION.

It will begin with a murmur – communication. We must talk to each other.

It will crescendo, slowly, into an opera of our choosing. But we must all be in agreement. Power comes from unity; discourse will only create a cacophony of displeasure. It would be truly pointless.

We must be like sirens; harmonious. We must sing so promisingly that only the most absurd would ignore us. Thus, we'll have the beginnings of our Revolution.

We might fail.

Sisyphus still slides back down his hill.

The candle will blow out.

Our hope will fracture.

It is risky. There are no promises of victory.

BUT

Sisyphus can pick himself up, ready to climb again.

A candle is meant to be relit over and over and over.

Our hope can mend like a broken heart.

Failure can be temporary, but only if you choose it to be.

We are on a time limit. Ten years until climate change is irreversible. We must prioritise our challenges, focus our efforts. Only then can we finally see our small changes stack up and show us the bigger picture we've struggled and persisted for. We just need to better our patience and our communication.

The choice is up to us:

we could give up –

let civilisation end.

We once thought the end of the world would be signalled with red skies.

The old Norse thought it was Ragnarök; when the gods battle giants.

A bubbling hatred spilling over into complete chaos.

A devastated Earth.

But that picture is all wrong, isn't it?

We'll just fizzle out.

Species will die out one by one.

And we'll argue – 'Oh it's just natural that things die out' – until we aren't around to argue anymore.

OR

Some of us could acknowledge we were wrong.

135

We could overcome our fear of humiliation – public and self-inflicted.

We could start acting, not just burning out at the planning stage. We could actually start to listen, and not just say we're listening. We could teach people how to process thought and philosophy. We could unite and accept diversity and differences. We could start listening to rationality.

We must overcome, but we cannot do that if we are throwing Molotovs back at the other side.

We must not fight as grotesquely as those who hurt us do. WE CAN DO BETTER.

Do you know what it feels like

to breathe brightly

with hope?

– Perhaps this 'thicker skin'

is a skin of dread,

layer upon layer

around my organs.

Squeezing.

It's been a while since I could breathe brightly.

Is it still possible?

A letter to the youth of Australia

Dear youth,

We know you are idealistic and want a society where we care for each other and care for our planet. As you have told us so many times, there is no planet B.

For so long you tried to get our attention to tell us that you did not believe in the society we are building and the future we are carving out for you. We watched your anxiety grow, and we gave you people to help you 'cope' with what was, in many ways, a sad society.

However, I am here to tell you there is hope. More and more people are listening, and we also want change. The pandemic has been a great wakeup call and it has made us look more closely at the society we have created, and it is clear we need a reset.

Through **The Heart's Language Project** (heartslanguage. com.au), we want to work for you and with you to create a fairer, kinder and more sustainable society.

We want to build a society where bitterness and hatred are not the norm, where people are put before profit, where cooperation and collaboration are encouraged as the way of doing business, and where looking after our environment is a top priority.

We are well aware that there are powerful people who do not want change because they benefit from the way things are, and we know that as individuals we cannot achieve a lot, but we also know that if we work together, we can be powerful and bring about changes in the areas we want in society. As social activist Arundhati Roy once said, *Another world is not only possible, she is on her way. On a quiet day, I can hear her breathing.*

We can get this done.

Yours in solidarity,

Jeanette Pritchard

Resources

Websites

This book is the beginning of a journey. The conversation generated by this book will continue on my webpage. I look forward to you all being involved.

theheartslanguage.com.au

Ripples of Hope – project websites

- Margaret Hepworth – The Ghandi Experiment: http://www.margarethepworth.com/
- Lea Trafford – Connecting conversations: https://connectingconversations.com.au
- Woman and Child Health Project, Jagriti Bhalai Kendra Society: https://womanandchildhealth.org
- The Liora Project: https://thelioraproject.com
- Guria: http://www.guriaindia.org; https://goodgriefproductions.com
- Clare Pritchard – Kindred Kindness: https://www.kindredkindness.org/what-we
- Donalea Patman – For the Love of Wildlife: https://fortheloveofwildlife.org.au/; https://natureneedsmore.org
- Judy Avisar – Three sides of the Coin: http://www.linkhc.org.au/three-sides-of-the-coin/

- Belinda Grooby – Tribe Monbulk Inc:
  https://www.facebook.com/tribemonbulkyouthgroup/
- Shakti Maclean – The Hills Food Frontier:
  https://thehillsfoodfrontier.org.au/

Mentoring programs

- Standing Tall mentoring program – Hamilton:
  www.standingtallhamilton.com.au
- Standing Tall mentoring program – Warrnambool:
  https://www.standingtalliw.com.au/
- BigBrothersBigSisters Australia:
  https://www.bigbrothersbigsisters.org.au/

Politics and political action

- https://www.aph.gov.au/About_Parliament/Parliamentary_
  Departments/Parliamentary_Library/Browse_by_Topic/
  Politicalparties
- https://www.getup.org.au/

Asset-based community development

- Cormac Russell Ted Talk:
  https://www.youtube.com/watch?v=a5xR4QB1ADw
- Nuture Development: www.nurturedevelopment.org; www.
  nurturedevelopment.org/blog
- Bank of Ideas: https://bankofideas.com.au/

Volunteering

- https://govolunteer.com.au/
- www.volunteer.com.au

Climate Change action

- https://www.climaterealityproject.org/training
- Friends of the Earth: https://www.melbournefoe.org.au/
- Climate change council: www.climatecouncil.org.au/

Others

- http://www.huffingtonpost.com.au/2017/04/11/mental-illness-is-still-on-the-rise-in-australian-youth-study-s_a_22034649/
- https://www.youthbeyondblue.com/footer/stats-and-facts
- https://headspace.org.au/news/new-abs-figures-youth-suicide/
- http://www.theage.com.au/comment/our-society-is-fraying-the-problem-starts-with-our-political-leaders-20170130-gu1xdh.html
- https://www.google.com.au/amp/www.independent.co.uk/news/world/americas/us-politics/london-attack-trump-sadiq-khan-us-mayors-thank-leadership-contrast-a7773981.html%3Famp
- https://www.theguardian.com/commentisfree/2017/feb/08/take-back-control-bottom-up-communities?CMP=fb_gu
- http://www.abc.net.au/news/2017-05-04/teachers-know-bigger-problems-classroom-gonski/8495584
- http://www.abc.net.au/news/2017-11-08/paradise-papers-why-we-lost-trust-in-institutions/9125944
- http://www.abc.net.au/news/2017-11-27/schools-at-crisis-point-mental-health-concerns-among-students/9192386
- http://www.abc.net.au/news/2018-03-15/gun-control-us-teenagers-could-finally-force-action/9551084
- https://www.theage.com.au/national/cheating-at-cricket-just-one-of-the-unthinkable-things-aussies-do-now-20180327-p4z6fc.html

- https://www.theguardian.com/australia-news/
  commentisfree/2018/dec/18/its-been-a-year-of-reckoning-for-
  banks-a-cricket-team-and-the-nation
- http://www.afr.com/news/politics/election/why-democracy-
  isnt-delivering-and-why-citizens-juries-will-20180117-
  h0k2gv#ixzz55X6iBYIr
- https://www.morningfuture.com/en/article/2019/04/26/
  empathy-happiness-school-denmark/601/
- https://www.ted.com/talks/katharine_wilkinson_how_
  empowering_women_and_girls_can_help_stop_global_
  warming
- https://www.couriermail.com.au/rendezview/the-anxiety-
  epidemic-gripping-our-kids/news-story/04b51d148f492f48b78e
  2c810ef340d0
- https://www.ted.com/talks/nicola_sturgeon_
  why_governments_should_prioritize_well_being/
  discussion?rss=172BB350-0206
- https://thinkequal.org/
- https://www.mindfulmomentsinedu.com/
  uploads/1/8/8/1/18811022/kindnesscurriculum.pdf

A personal reflective exercise

1. What are your main hopes for:

    - Society in general?
    - Your local community?
    - Your personal life?

2. What are the main challenges (2–3) that are being put in front or you?

3. What are your main sources of energy at the present time?:

    - Where does that energy come from?
    - What are the situations where you feel your heart opening?
    - When do you feel the energy coming through you?

4. If you could look at you above at what you do in a day, what is it you are trying to do:

    - At a personal level?
    - At a community level?
    - At a societal level?

5. At each level:

    - What needs to be let go of?
    - What needs to be learnt?
    - What are the things you have accomplished?
    - What things are still possible?
    - What are the questions and the doubts you live with?

6. Go to the person you were as a child/young person. Through those eyes, observe your current self. What would you say?:

    - Observation
    - Advice
    - Appreciation

7. Fast forward to the end of your life. Ask yourself, what is your footprint?

8. If you would fully commit to bringing that vision into fruition, what would you need to let go of?:
   - Assumptions
   - Behaviours
   - Attitudes

9. What could you take from that vision that would make it real in the next three months?

10. Who are five people you want to connect with?

11. What actions are needed to take it from an idea to a realisation?

Heart connection meditation by Cheryne Blom

This meditation has five parts:

1. Focus on the here and now
2. Mindful breathing
3. Body relaxation
4. Heart connection
5. Creative visualisation

This is a meditation that helps you connect with your heart centre and the energy in your heart. Often, we focus on the world outside of us. We look for validation, recognition and completion outside of ourselves. This meditation takes you into the essence of you. The essence within your heart. Your true self. Your authentic self, and the heart of who you are. Not only is this meditation a place to take you into your inner world, but it also helps you to soothe turbulent emotions. It can help you regulate your feelings. This helps you connect to your internal wisdom and intuition. Listen to the gentle whispers of that voice. It will guide you to your true path.

To begin, make sure you are sitting or lying down in a comfortable position. Make sure that your phone is switched off and there will be no interruptions. Start by closing your eyelids gently. Notice that there is a space behind your eyelids and bring your awareness to that space. This allows you to come into the here and now and focus on the present moment. This will help you to still your thoughts, to distract you from your to-do list and to focus on the world within you.

As you focus on that space behind your eyelids, take note of what is in that space. Imagine that it is your own internal movie screen. That screen reflects your own inner world.

Take note of what is on your screen. It may be completely blank. There may be shapes or colours. It may be still, or it may be moving. Simply observe what is on your screen. That space represents your internal world. Your internal landscape. Imagine travelling into that space as you imagine travelling into your body. Become fully present with your body, in the here and now, and feel the sensations in your body.

As you are tuning into your body, travel deeper and locate your breath. Feel the gentle flow of your breath. Feel the inhale breath rise and the exhale breath fall. Take a few deep breaths, observing the rhythm of your breath. With every breath cycle, allow your breath to relax. Allow your breath to soften the entire body.

Now, bring your awareness to your breath in the centre of your heart. Feel it deep in the centre of your body. Feel your breath moving in and out of your heart space. As you breathe in, feel your breath enter the heart. As you breathe out, feel your breath flow out of the heart. As your breath flows out of the heart, feel the heart open. Feel it expand.

Imagine travelling all the way into your heart. Right into the depths of your being. Notice that there is a beautiful and warm flickering flame. It is like a pilot light that is flickering deep within you. Connect with this beautiful light. Feel its presence. Feel its warmth. Feel its flow.

Notice that this light is connected to everything that powers the universe. The force that is powering the universe is bringing life into you through that flame. You can feel the connection to everything in the universe. Bring your awareness to that flickering flame. Feel your breath in the depths of that flame. As you are tuning into the flame, notice how it feels. What are the qualities of that flame? Tune-in to this gentle essence within you. Imagine your breath is powering this flame. As you breathe in you can feel the flame rise. As you exhale you can feel your breath fanning through your heart space.

Imagine that you have a dial, like a dimmer switch. Just imagine turning up the dial and imagine the flame growing and expanding deep in your breath. Imagine the flame rising, becoming warmer and expanding through your body. Feel the warmth. Feel this light expand. Use your exhale breath to send it all around your body. Turn up the dial and observe the light expanding all around your body.

You can feel this beautiful essence warming you and expanding through your body. Feel the qualities of this light – the wisdom and the intuition. Feel its power and confidence. The courage. The strength. Feel those qualities in the depth of that flame.

Now imagine turning that dial up even further. Watch this beautiful light. Observe a golden light shining out of your body, shining brightly out onto the world. Feel its authentic essence. Feel the heart of you shining out onto the world around you, shining brightly onto everyone in your world.

Feel your light uplifting those around you, sharing love and peace. Sharing hope, empathy, action, relationships and trust. This is the power of your heart. This is the power of love.

Enjoy this for a few moments. When you are ready, slowly open your eyes.

Cheryne Blom

Author of *The Courage to Be You*

www.cheryneblom.com

Endnotes

Introduction

1   John Marsden, *The Art of Growing up* (Australia: Pan Macmillan, 2019), 175.

Part I, Chapter 1

2   'Joint statement', Australian Medical Association, accessed 30 July, 2020, https://ama.com.au/media/joint-statement-covid-19-impact-likely-lead-increased-rates-suicide-and-mental-illness

3   'The Five Year Mental Health Report has launched', Mission Australia, accessed 30 July, 2020, https://www.missionaustralia.com.au/news-blog/blog/the-five-year-youth-mental-health-report-has-launched

4   Henrietta Cook, 'Principals sound the alarm on mental illness in primary school kids', *The Age*, 2 April, 2019.

5   'Australian Attitudes to Young People Survey Media Release', ARACY, https://www.aracy.org.au/publications-resources/command/download_file/id/211/filename/34_01_July_2012_-_Australian_children_defy_stereotypes.pdf

6   'Rates of suicide continue to increase for young Australians', Orygen, *The National Centre of Excellence in Youth Mental Health Newsletter*, www.orygen.org.au, 26 September, 2019.

7   Stephanie Dalzell, 'Push to get wellbeing counsellors into schools as mental health bill costs Australia billions', *ABC News*, 31 October, 2019.

8   'Model for positive education', Geelong Grammar School, accessed 30 July, 2020, https://www.ggs.vic.edu.au/Positive-Education2/Model-for-Positive-Education

9   John Marsden, *The Art of Growing Up* (Australia: Pan Macmillan, 2019), 373.

10   *Q&A*, ABC, 9 September, 2019.

11 Hayek material in McKnight, D., *Beyond Right and Left: New Politics and the Culture Wars* (Sydney: Allen and Unwin, 2003), 66.

12 Ibid, p.70.

13 Ibid, p.71.

14 Will Kenton, 'Trickle-Down Theory', Investopedia, 14 July, 2019, accessed 30 July, 2020, https://www.investopedia.com/terms/t/trickledowntheory.asp

15 Stephen Bartholomeusz, 'Ken Henry ponders the state of capitalism – and agrees it's not pretty', *Sydney Morning Herald*, 28 November, 2018.

16 Sharon Beder, Richard Gosden and Wendy Varney, *This Little Kiddy Went to Market: The Corporate Capture of Childhood* (Sydney: University of New South Wales Press, 2009), 40.

17 Johann Hari, *Lost Connections: Uncovering the Real Causes of Depression – and the Unexpected Solutions* (USA: Bloomsbury, 2018), 100.

18 Reg Bailey, 'Letting Children be Children', Department for Education, accessed 30 July, 2020, https://assets.publishing.service.gov.uk/government/uploads/system/uploads/attachment_data/file/175418/Bailey_Review.pdf

19 E Rush and A La Nauze, 'Corporate Paedophilia: Sexualisation of children in Australia', The Australia Institute, 1 October, 2006.

20 Joel Bakan, *The Corporation: The Pathological Pursuit of Profit and Power* (Canada: Penguin, 2004), 119.

21 Melissa Davey, Lisa Cox and Stuart MacFarlane, 'Victorian aged care leak shows Melbourne home "begging" for staff after coronavirus outbreak', *The Guardian*, 15 August, 2020.

22 Michael Evans, 'Harvey: charity not so sweet', *Sydney Morning Herald*, 21 November, 2008.

23 Van Badham, 'The "prosperity doctrine" and neoliberal Jesusing, Scott Morrison-style', *The Guardian*, 29 August, 2018.

24 Adam Carey, 'Jewish boys taunted in shocking cases of anti-Semitic bullying at Melbourne schools', *The Age*, 3 October, 2019.

25 Rob Harris, '"Sitting ducks": Federal MPs raise alarm over personal safety fears', *Sydney Morning Herald*, 27 August, 2019.

26 Ibid.

27 Natassia Chrysanthos and Rob Harris, 'Alan Jones tells Scott Morrison to "shove a sock down throat" of Jacinda Ardern', *Sydney Morning Herald*, 15 August, 2019.

28 Danah Zohar and Ian Marshall, *Spiritual Capital: Wealth We Can Live By* (London: Bloomsbury Publishing Plc, 2004), 13.

29 Sumeyya Ilanbey and Tom Cowie, 'Boys from St Kevin's College filmed chanting sexist song', *The Age*, 22 October, 2019.

30 Kristian Silva and James Oaten, 'Kevin's College principal condemns "foolish" students after sexist chant repeated in public', *ABC Radio Melbourne*, 25 October 2019.

31 Ibid.

32 Rohan Smith, 'Former student at St Kevin's College blames "insidious, hyper-masculine" culture for sexist tram chant', *News.com.au*, 23 October, 2019.

33 Kristian Silva and James Oaten, 'Kevin's College principal condemns "foolish" students after sexist chant repeated in public', *ABC Radio Melbourne*, 25 October 2019.

34 Ibid.

35 Emma Jane, 'There's a reason St Kevin's College boys started a sexist chant: society is geared against women', *ABC News*, 24 October, 2019.

36 David Leser, *Women, men & the whole damn thing* (Sydney: Allen and Unwin, 2019), ix.

37 Ibid, p.xii.

38 Ibid, p.5.

39 Ibid, p.3.

40 Ibid, p.4.

41 Ibid.

42 Ibid.

43 'Ending violence against women', UN Women, accessed 30 July, 2020, https://www.unwomen.org/en/what-we-do/ending-violence-against-women

44 The Australian Women Donors Network, accessed 30 July, 2020, http://www.womendonors.org.au/

45   David Leser, *Women, men & the whole damn thing* (Sydney: Allen and Unwin, 2019), 11.

46   Ibid.

47   The Australian Women Donors Network, accessed 30 July, 2020, http://www.womendonors.org.au/

48   Ibid.

49   David Leser, *Women, men & the whole damn thing* (Sydney: Allen and Unwin, 2019), 110.

50   'Women and the Workplace – Fast Facts', The Australian Women Donors Network, accessed 30 July, 2020, http://www.womendonors.org.au/uplaods/fast-facts/12414_Women_and_the_Workplace_v2.pdf

51   Peter Ryan, 'Women going backwards at the top of corporate Australia', *ABC News*, 10 September, 2019.

52   The Australian Women Donors Network, accessed 15 August, 2020, http://www.womendonors.org.au/

53   David Leser, *Women, men & the whole damn thing* (Sydney: Allen and Unwin, 2019), 103.

54   Ibid, p.14.

55   Ibid, p.267.

56   Ibid, p.266.

57   Ibid, p.270.

58   Ibid.

59   Ibid, p.137.

60   'Why I'm done trying to be "man enough"', TED Talks, accessed 30 July, 2020, https://www.ted.com/talks/justin_baldoni_why_i_m_done_trying_to_be_man_enough?

61   David Leser, *Women, men & the whole damn thing* (Sydney: Allen and Unwin, 2019), 136.

62   Ibid, p.157.

63   Hayley Gleeson, 'Jess Hill's mission to understand abusive men', *ABC News,* 23 June, 2019.

64   Jane Gilmour, 'The complexity of male suicide', *The Saturday Paper*, 12 October, 2019.

65 Bell Hooks, accessed 15 August, 2020, https://en.wikiquote.org/wiki/Bell_hooks

Part I, Chapter 2

66 *Q&A*, ABC, 21 July, 2019, accessed 30 July 2020, https://www.abc.net.au/qanda/

67 Arundhati Roy, 'The Pandemic Is a Portal', *YES! Magazine*, 17 April, 2020.

68 Katherine Trebeck and Jeremy Williams, *The Economics of Arrival: Ideas for a grown up economy* (Bristol, UK: Policy Press, 2019), 20.

69 Johann Hari, *Lost Connections: Uncovering the Real Causes of Depression – and the Unexpected Solutions* (USA: Bloomsbury, 2018), 95–96.

70 AVAAZ email 14 May, 2020, 'Something beautiful is happening', Mike Baillie, Avaaz avaaz@avaaz.org.

71 'Bourke Street attack first responders extend emotional thank you to selfless civilians', *9NEWS*, 3 February, 2017.

72 Adrian Ward, 'Scientists Probe Human Nature – and Discover We Are Good, After All', *Scientific American*, 20 November, 2012.

73 Katherine Trebeck and Jeremy Williams, *The Economics of Arrival: Ideas for a grown up economy* (Bristol, UK: Policy Press, 2019), 141.

74 David Leser, *Women, men & the whole damn thing* (Sydney: Allen and Unwin, 2019), 294.

75 'The Equality of Men and Women', The Bahá'í Faith, accessed 30 July, 2020, https://www.bahai.org/beliefs/universal-peace/articles-resources/the-equality-men-women

76 David Leser, *Women, men & the whole damn thing* (Sydney: Allen and Unwin, 2019), 284.

77 Ibid, pp.274–5.

Part I, Chapter 3

78 Email from Helena Norberg, 6 July, 2020, 'The truth about globalisation and its destructive path', https://www.localfutures.org/about/who-we-are/helena-norberg-hodge/

79   Hugh Mackay, 'The state of the nation starts in your street', *The Conversation*, 2 February, 2017.

80   'Dying Alone: An interview with Eric Klinenberg', *Chicago Press, accessed 30 July, 2020,* https://press.uchicago.edu/Misc/Chicago/443213in.html

81   George Monbiot, 'This is how people can truly take back control: from the bottom up', *The Guardian*, 8 February, 2017.

82   'Asset-based community development', Wikipedia, accessed 30 July, 2020, https://en.wikipedia.org/wiki/Asset-based_community_development

83   Lao Tzu quote, accessed 30 July, 2020, https://www.goodreads.com/quotes/215411-go-to-the-people-live-with-them-learn-from-them

Part I, Chapter 4

84   School Strike 4 Climate Australia, https://www.schoolstrike4climate.com/

85   'Transcript: Greta Thunberg's Speech At The U.N. Climate Action Summit', 23 September, 2019, accessed 30 July, 2020, https://www.npr.org/2019/09/23/763452863/transcript-greta-thunbergs-speech-at-the-u-n-climate-action-summit

86   'The Safe Climate Declaration', NCE Summit, accessed 30 July, 2020, https://www.climateemergencysummit.org/declaration/

87   Lisa Cox, 'Former fire chiefs warn Australia unprepared for escalating climate threat', *The Guardian*, 10 April, 2019.

88   James Fernyhough, 'Government buried climate risk action plan', *Financial Review,* 11 January, 2020.

89   David Crowe, 'Deputy PM slams people raising climate change in relation to NSW bushfires', *Sydney Morning Herald*, 11 November, 2019.

90   'Malcolm Turnbull lashes out at former colleagues, Murdoch media over climate denial', *The New Daily*, 16 January, 2020.

91   Jim Waterson, 'James Murdoch criticises father's news outlets for climate crisis denial', *The Guardian*, 15 January, 2020.

92   Michael Brissenden, 'Climate Wars', *Four Corners*, ABC, 18 May, 2020.

93 'The Safe Climate Declaration', NCE Summit, accessed 30 July, 2020, https://www.climateemergencysummit.org/declaration/

94 Ibid.

95 Adam Morton, 'Gas "completely dominated" discussions about Covid-19 recovery, commission advisor says', *The Guardian*, 13 June, 2020.

96 Simon Rogers, 'Bobby Kennedy on GDP: "measure everything except that which is worthwhile"', *The Guardian*, 24 May, 2012.

97 Emma Charlton, 'New Zealand has unveiled its first "well-being" budget', World Economic Forum, 30 May, 2019.

98 Katherine Trebeck and Jeremy Williams, *The Economics of Arrival: Ideas for a grown up economy* (Bristol, UK: Policy Press, 2019), 19.

99 Lauren Ferri and Alana Mazzoni, '"Just call Jacinda": Lisa Wilkinson pens extraordinary open letter to ScoMo begging him to "start the healing" by asking New Zealand's prime minister for advice', *Daily Mail Australia*, 19 May, 2019.

100 Chris Bramwell, 'Jacinda Ardern on US breakfast TV show: Joy of parenthood "far surpassed expectations"', *RNZ*, 25 September, 2018.

101 'Time to Care', Oxfam, accessed 30 July, 2020, https://oxfamilibrary.openrepository.com/bitstream/handle/10546/620928/bp-time-to-care-inequality-200120-en.pdf

102 Ross Gittins, 'One of the most exciting discoveries in economics pays a happiness dividend', *Sydney Morning Herald*, 28 August, 2019.

103 Ibid.

104 Ibid.

105 Aboriginal Heritage Office, accessed 11 September 2020, https://www.aboriginalheritage.org/

106 Amy McQuire, 'There cannot be 432 victims and no perpetrators...' *The Saturday Paper*, 6 June, 2020.

Part II, Chapter 5

107 James Doty, *Into the Magic Shop: A Neurosurgeon's Quest to Discover the Mysteries of the Brain and the Secrets of the Heart* (New York: Penguin Random House, 2016), 95.

108 Lew Childe and Howard Martin, *The Heartmath Solution* (New York: Harper Collins, 1999), 7.

109 Ibid, p.8.

110 Ibid.

111 Ibid.

112 Ibid, p.10.

113 Ibid.

114 Ibid, p.13.

115 Hugh MacKay, *Beyond Belief* (Australia: Pan McMillan, 2016), 245–248.

116 Matt Noffs, 'New spirituality transcends boundaries of belief', *Sydney Morning Herald*, 8 March, 2012.

117 Wayside Chapel, https://www.waysidechapel.org.au/

Part II, Chapter 6

118 *Q&A*, ABC, 29 July, 2019, https://www.abc.net.au/qanda/

119 Larry Brentro, Martin Brokenleg and Steve Van Bockern, *Reclaiming Youth at Risk: Our Hope for the Future* (Bloomington, Indiana: National Education Service, 1990).

120 James Doty, *Into the Magic Shop: A Neurosurgeon's Quest to Discover the Mysteries of the Brain and the Secrets of the Heart* (New York: Penguin Random House, 2016), 95.

121 Leigh Sales, *Any Ordinary Day* (Australia: Random House, 2018), 231.

122 'Jacinda Ardern's speech at Christchurch memorial – full transcript', *The Guardian*, 29 March, 2019.

123 Jacqueline Howard, 'Psychologists Reveal One Of The Best Ways To Boost Your Mood', *Huffington Post*, 25 April, 2016.

124 Ibid.

125 Ibid.

126 Jill Stark, 'Changing the world and ourselves through compassion', *The Age*, 11 April, 2015.

127 Richard Davidson, 'A Neuroscientist on Love and Learning' Podcast *On Being*, 14 February, 2019.

128 'Empathy? In Denmark they're learning it in school', Morning FUTURE, 26 April, 2019.

129 Ibid.

130 Hugh Van Cuylenburg, 'Three steps to resilience', *The Weekend Australian Magazine*, 22 November, 2019.

131 'March for Our Lives', Wikipedia, accessed 30 July, 2020, https://en.wikipedia.org/wiki/March_for_Our_Lives

132 Ibid.

133 Project Drawdown, https://www.drawdown.org

134 P2P Foundation, https://p2pfoundation.net/

135 Zameena Mejia, 'Harvard's study of adult life reveals how you can be happier and more successful', *CNBC*, 20 March, 2018.

136 Eryk Bagshaw, 'Kenneth Hayne: Trust in politics has "been destroyed"', *Sydney Morning Herald*, 7 August, 2019.

137 Annabel Crabb, 'Australia Talks National Survey reveals what Australians are most worried about' *ABC News*, 8 October, 2019.

138 Ibid.

Part III, Chapter 7

139 Kon Karapanagiotidis, *The Power of Hope* (Sydney: Harper Collins, 2018), 100.

140 Bill Bostock, 'An intensive-care expert broke down just how contagious the coronavirus is, showing how one person could end up infecting 59,000 in a snowball effect', *Business Insider*, 23 March, 2020.

141 Alyssa Yeo, 'The Story of Two Wolves', Urban Balance, accessed 30 July, 2020, https://urbanbalance.com/the-story-of-two-wolves/

Part III, Chapter 8

142 'The Politics We Have – The Politics We Need', Pearls and Irritations, 22 November, 2019.

143 Kon Karapanagiotidis, *The Power of Hope* (Sydney: Harper Collins, 2018), 260.

144 GetUp!, https://www.getup.org.au/

145 Ibid.

146 Jeremy Heimans and Henry Timms, *New Power* (Australia: Pan Macmillan, 2018).

147 Ibid.

148 Holly Wainwright, 'Greta Thunberg is not an ordinary 16-year-old. And it scares her bullies senseless', MamaMia, 25 September, 2019.

149 Ibid.

150 Ibid.

151 Jennifer O'Connell, 'Why is Greta Thunberg so triggering for certain men?' *Irish Times*, 7 September, 2019.

152 Bank Australia, 'How millennials are driving the rise of conscious capitalism', *The Guardian*, 28 February, 2019.

153 Ibid.

154 From Wikipedia: Woke, accessed 11 September 2020, https://en.wikipedia.org/wiki/Woke

155 Marian Cheik-Hussein, 'Tiffany & Co uses ads to tell the PM to fight climate change', *AdNews*, 13 January, 2020.

156 Lucy Dean, 'Optus, Vodafone match Telstra, waives fireys' phone bills', *Yahoo Finance*, 3 January, 2020.

157 Nature needs more, accessed 11 September 2020, https://natureneedsmore.org/re-inventing-magnificence/

158 GreenBiz, accessed 11 September 2020, https://www.greenbiz.com/article/shareholders-put-pressure-corporate-climate-action

159 'Future of local government project', Municipal Association of Victoria, accessed 30 July, 2020, https://www.mav.asn.au/what-we-do/sector-development/future-of-local-government

Part III, Chapter 9

160 Robert F. Kennedy quote, GoodReads, accessed 30 July, 2020, https://www.goodreads.com/quotes/705426-each-time-a-man-stands-up-for-an-ideal-or

161 Brené Brown, *Rising Strong* (UK: Penguin Random House, 2015), 7.

Bibliography

Bakan, Joel. *The Corporation. The Pathological Pursuit of Profit and Power.* Canada: Penguin, 2004.

Bancroft, Jack. *Mentoring: The key to a fairer world.* Victoria, Australia: Hardie Grant Books, 2018.

Beder, Sharon. *This Little Kiddy Went to Market: The Corporate Capture of Childhood.* Sydney: University of New South Wales Press, 2009.

Brentro, Larry, Brokenleg, Martin and Van Bockern, Steve. *Reclaiming Youth at Risk,* Bloomington, Indiana: National Education Service, 1990.

Brown Brené. *Rising Strong.* London: Penguin Random House, 2015.

Childe, Lew and Martin, Howard. *The Heartmath Solution.* New York: Harper Collins, 1999.

Diers, Jim. *Neighbor Power: Building Community The Seattle Way.* Seattle: University of Washington Press, 2006.

Doty, James. *Into the Magic Shop: A Neurosurgeon's Quest to Discover the Mysteries of the Brain and the Secrets of the Heart.* New York: Penguin Random House, 2016.

Fredrickson, Barbara. *Creating Happiness and Health in Moments of Connection.* New York: Penguin, 2014.

Hari, Johann. *Lost Connections: Uncovering the Real Causes of Depression – and the Unexpected Solutions* USA: Bloomsbury, 2018.

Leser, David. *Women, men & the whole damn thing.* Sydney: Allen and Unwin, 2019.

Marsden, John. *The Art of Growing Up.* Australia: Pan Macmillan, 2019.

McKay, Hugh. *Beyond Belief.* Australia: Pan McMillan, 2016.

McKnight, David. *Beyond Right and Left: New Politics and the Culture Wars.* Sydney: Allen and Unwin, 2003.

Monbiot, George. *Out of the Wreckage: A New Politics for an Age of Crisis.* London: Verso Books, 2017.

159

Sales, Leigh. *Any Ordinary Day.* Australia: Random House, 2018.

Trebeck, Katherine and Williams, Jeremy. *The Economics of Arrival*: *Ideas for a grown up economy.* Bristol, UK: Policy Press Bristol, 2019.

Zohar, Danah and Marshall, Ian. *Spiritual Capital: Wealth We Can Live By.* London: Bloomsbury Publishing Plc, 2004.

Lightning Source UK Ltd.
Milton Keynes UK
UKHW011013231120
373921UK00002B/528